SO YOU THINK THE BIBLE IS CONFUSING

FUN FACTS, HELPFUL HINTS, AND ANSWERS
TO SOME OF THE MOST COMMON QUESTIONS

SHARON ROSE

ISBN 978-1-68517-930-4 (paperback)
ISBN 978-1-68517-931-1 (digital)

Christian Faith Publishing
832 Park Avenue
Meadville, PA 16335
www.christianfaithpublishing.com

Disclosure: The information and contents of this book is correct to the best of my knowledge. Due to ongoing research and new findings, some information may change. However, the Scripture will not change.

Printed in the United States of America

F un facts, helpful hints, and answers to some of the most confusing questions. This book is easy to read and easy to understand.

DEDICATION

A world of thanks to my husband, Sherman, for his patience while I was taking up all the space at the kitchen table with all of my books, papers, pens, pencils, and notebooks. I am grateful for his understanding during all the time I spent at my desk writing, studying, and researching. I also want to thank him for his thoughts on some things about the Bible that seem to confuse people.

My most wonderful beautiful daughter, for her encouragement, feedback, suggestions, patience, knowledge, support, resources, advice, faith in me, her time, her honesty, for believing in me, and most of all her love.

My beautiful granddaughter for showing me how to create my own illustrations, her patience and her loving heart.

My dear niece, Melinda, for her input, her suggestions, her lending ear, her shoulder, her honesty, her support, her ideas, for believing in me, and her love.

Special thanks to all of my family and friends who gave me support, ideas, and suggestions. I love you all.

I also want to thank the family members who were skeptical, who laughed, *poked fun*, and did not believe in me. You gave me even more reason and desire out of love to write this book and to show "Greater is the One Living inside of me, than he who is Living in the World" (1 John 4:4).

I pray that God opens your heart and mind to get a better understanding of who He is and enjoy His story through the Bible, His book.

Special thanks to the pastors, Bible teachers, and leaders for having a big impact on my biblical education.

Pastor Tom Pendergrass, Urbancrest Baptist Church, Lebanon, Ohio

Pastor Renaut van der Riet, Mosaic Church, Winter Garden, Florida

My Messianic Bible Study Teacher and Leader, The Villages, Florida

I sincerely appreciate all the ladies who have been a leader in my many Bible studies. I also want to say thanks to the many ladies who shared in the learning experiences during our time together in Christian fellowship.

Thanks to Pastor Doss Estep, Mission Pastor, for making it possible for me to join the educational trip to Israel and for encouraging me to go on the mission trip to Venezuela. You are also an inspiration for many more of my journeys, such as disaster relief and mission trips that were local, national, and international.

Most of all, I thank my Dear Lord, Jesus Christ, for placing these wonderful Christ-followers, Holy Spirit-filled people in my life during the walk of deepening my faith in the Lord God Almighty.

CONTENTS

WELCOME

I recently read an article from publishersweekly.com (by Jim Milliot, January 14, 2021) that there is a boom on sales for self-improvement type of books. So I went searching and found a list on Amazon.com under Self-Help that included at least twenty-eight different types of how-to books, self-help guides, books on self-improvement/self-development, top ten ways to do this or that, how to change your life, personal growth, inspirational books, and more.

Those books are written by people. The information in the book cannot and will not help you unless you read it and apply those instructions as directed. The words will not jump off the pages and make you do what the author intended the book to help you do. Now that is the same concept with the Bible. God is the ultimate author of the Bible. He used many people to write the books. The words in those books cannot help you just by reading them, you will need to apply the instructions that are provided to your daily life in order for the *self-help* to work. You are not doing this by *yourself*. You do have the author of the book guiding you, so you are not really alone when reading your self-help books. You also have God as the author of His book to be there with you as you read and apply His *instructions*.

PREFACE

Before we get started on our journey, let's stop for a few moments to prepare. Most of the time when we are getting ready to go on a trip or journey, we get our things together, which usually means we need to get our thoughts together first. So let us do that. Close your eyes, and ask God to open your heart and mind as you travel through this book in preparation for the journey you will be taking in your Bible. If you are not comfortable praying, or you don't know God personally, just stop for a few minutes and give some thought about reading this book and keep an open mind. I pray that after you have read this book, you will have gained some clarity. Some of your questions or thoughts that you have are a little bit clearer.

My goal is to write in simple words, terms, and language so people from all stages of life or walk with God will be able to read with confidence and no longer be afraid to open up the Bible. If you have had questions, if you've wanted to read the Bible but you've felt confused and frustrated, or if you are comfortable reading the Bible but want to know more about it, then this book is for you. I pray that God will bless you with the desire to know Him through His word.

This book is not intended to answer all of your questions. It is just some of the basic answers to the most commonly asked questions. You may find information that you didn't know to ask. You didn't know what you didn't know. After you read this book and become a little more comfortable and a little less confused, start reading your Bible. Then supplement that reading with well-known, trusted authors and study books that are biblically correct. Please do not rely on everything that you read, see, or hear from social media sources. Some may be biblically correct, and some may not. I recommend doing some research on your own or get some help from people whom you know and trust. There are some trustworthy sources listed in the Recommended Resources provided later in this book. Always refer to your Bible. When I use the word Bible in this book, I will always be referring to the God-inspired Old and New Testament, which many know as the Holy Bible.

Over the years, I have been listening to people express why they don't read or study the Bible. That caused sadness in my heart. I know it was a God-thing that led me to write this book. I started praying about it and then I prayed some more. The idea continued to surface. I know God was going to tug at my heart until I said yes. Have you ever had a thought or idea that just kept coming to mind? Did you set it aside thinking, *Where did that idea come from?* Maybe after you did put some serious thought into it, you approached the idea and decided to go for it. Maybe successful or maybe not, at least you tried. So now, I am going for it and praying it will succeed in helping you better understand the Bible.

There are different versions of the Bible. For the sake of variety and to give you an idea of how different versions of the Bible use different words while keeping the same meaning, I will be using several versions of the Bible throughout this book. What does version mean? "A particular form of something that is slightly different from the other forms of the same thing" (Cambridge Dictionary) https://dictionary.cambridge.org/us/dictionary/english/version. We will be covering what it means to use different versions later in the chapter called Which Version of the Bible Should I Read?

This book should not be confused with a Bible study or Sunday school lesson. This book is intended to get you comfortable and less confused about the Bible so that you can enjoy a Bible study, enjoy Sunday school lesson, or enjoy your quiet time alone. You will have a lot more knowledge and insight when you finish this book. I know you will probably have a few *Ah-ha* moments. Or find yourself saying, "I did not know that" or "so that's what that means."

HOW I MET THE BIBLE: A SHORT MEMOIR

When I first discovered or physically saw a bible, I was probably six or seven years old. Honestly I don't remember how old, I just know that I was little. And I mean little like in size. Whether it was at my Granny Rosie's house in Pine Knot, Kentucky, or our apartment (tenement style) in downtown, I mean Over-The-Rhine downtown, Cincinnati, Ohio. I could still picture that Bible in my mind. It was large. It looked like it would be heavier than a Sears and Roebuck catalog. Well, I knew it was too heavy for me to pick up. A few of you who are reading this know what I'm talking about. Yeah, I saw you grinning.

Anyway, it seemed overwhelming and a little scary. No, it was a lot scary. Something about it seemed sacred, and maybe kids shouldn't touch it. But of course out of curiosity, I finally opened the front cover and then started turning one page at a time. Wow, those pages were beautiful, so full of very detailed and colorful pictures. And then as I continued to turn the pages, I came upon some very ugly and scary pages. It was pictures of the devil and fire. I was somewhat confused by that. Why would this beautiful book have all those ugly pictures in it? I didn't understand why until later in life when I actually started discovering more of the Bible.

I was in about the third or fourth grade when we moved from downtown Cincinnati to a *suburb* known as Fairmount. While attending the elementary school, I remembered every Wednesday we walked to a church and had *church school.* Isn't that awesome? I didn't think we had any Bibles, but we did have fun while we were taught some Bible stories. We learned about Adam and Eve, Noah and the ark with all the animals, and a baby named Moses found in a basket. Then there was this giant sea that opened up right down the middle so that hundreds of people could run to the other side to get away from some bad soldiers. The best story was about baby Jesus in a manger (that was a bed of straw), Mary and Joseph (Jesus's mom and dad), a few kings who brought presents, some really cute baby sheep, and a camel and a donkey. Plus the big star in the sky. Those were the stories that I remember the most.

Early in my childhood years, I found myself having the desire to read everything that had words. Read, read, read! I loved reading and still do. My Aunt Judy always had lots of books to read. She was my reading inspiration. I couldn't wait to go to visit her. I was a little nerd. Yes, folks, don't laugh. It's true. I was a very quiet little girl back then. Some folks who knew me then would say I am a little more outspoken now. I am assuming that those of you who are reading this and laughing probably know me personally. If you don't know me, it's okay. I'm sure you know someone in your life who was shy and rarely talked at all, and now you can't get them to stop. I am sharing this because it will give you some insight on my personality as it is being revealed while you are reading through this book. Well, enough about that.

When I was approximately twelve years old, we moved to a different *suburb* called Lower Price Hill. I was invited to ride a little Sunday school bus to a small church in Newport, Kentucky. The most profound and disheartening memory from that experience was the fact that I was never taught anything in this church from the Bible beyond heaven and hell. You had to have the *Holy Ghost* in order to speak in *tongues*. And if you didn't *speak in tongues* or have the *Holy Ghost*, you weren't *saved*.

I thought I was saved. That was confusing. I didn't know what that meant. I was so happy and thankful when I later found out the Bible does not say that at all. (The Biblical meaning of *tongues* and *Holy Ghost* are listed in Definitions and Descriptions later in this book.) We did learn a few things about God and Satan. I am so grateful to our Lord God that this personal experience did not scare me away from Christianity, like it did for other people that I know. The Holy Spirit is God in spiritual form, given to us to guide us in our daily lives. The Holy Spirit was not given by God to scare people away.

The best thing that came from attending that church was that my mom started going back to church after many years. She rededicated her life to the Lord and never turned back. She continued to walk with God all the way to heaven. Everyone remembered her long heartfelt prayers and her deep, loving heart. My mom was the beginning of my spiritual journey.

While we were living in Price Hill, the family next door also became very influential in my Christian walk. I guess I really didn't realize it at the time because I was still young and didn't understand the real meaning of being a Christian.

A few years later, we moved away to an area called Upper Price Hill. That was during my early teen years and that was when I got my first job. I babysat our neighbors' five kids to make money. With my .50 cents an hour, I joined a book club. I was not sure why I didn't buy a Bible but I didn't. I wish I had. Not much was happening with the Bible in those early teen years for me, just reading other stuff, going to school, and trying to be a good kid. (I did learn later on that just being good doesn't mean you go to heaven.)

Remember the family that I mentioned who influenced my Christian walk? Well, they became my in-laws when I married their son, the *boy next door*. I got my very first Bible, the King James Version, from my mother-in-law, Nell Barnes. (She signed it Mom #2. I still have it and refer to it often.) Here is where I started getting more interested in reading the Bible even though it was still confusing. It was exciting now to learn about what was actually in the Bible and not just what people tell you. And by the way, it was not scary anymore.

While I am here talking about my in-laws, I really wanted to share about the time when I lived with them and saw how they lived out the Bible. I am sure you would agree that you really get to know people when you live with them. This was God's gift to me. What a pleasure it was to see real godly love. Don't get me wrong, I am not implying they were perfect but close. Every day and at every dinner time, Sam, my father-in-law, or Nell always gave thanks before dinner. Not only was the prayer about giving thanks for our food, it was about thanking God for all of our blessings. Also in the prayer, they asked God to forgive us for our daily actions that were against God's will. The prayer usually ended with asking prayers for others in their circumstances which God knows about. Then the prayer ended with a hearty *amen.*

Being human, people get angry. During the time I lived with them, the most harsh words that I remember ever came out of Sam's mouth when he was angry at Nell was, "Nell, you are skating on thin ice." What an example. I do believe it was totally the love of God in their hearts and the knowledge of God's word and instructions that He gave us in the Bible that Nell and Sam were able to live a godly life. They lived out the Bible every day. They weren't just *Sunday Christians.* I received such a blessing living there. I watched them read the Bible. I watched them apply the teachings of the Bible. I watched them both every Sunday and Wednesday drive separate cars to church just so they could pick up others who couldn't drive themselves to church. They never complained about *going out of their way* or *how much gas cost.* It was not that they didn't have problems, it was how they handled the problems that made the difference. I am sure that was the teachings from the Holy Bible.

Let's fast forward to my adult years. As part of my continuing walk through the Bible and my Christian journey, I was invited to attend Urbancrest Baptist Church. I love this church, the pastor, the missions, the people, and the love that I received. I believed in miracles, and I got to experience many of them while I was a member of this church. One of them was when God blessed me with the privilege of going to Israel on an educational tour in 2008 with the mission team at Urbancrest Church.

While we were in Israel, I could actually see, touch, smell, hear, emotionally feel, and experience the Bible as I watched it come to life. That trip sure did confirm what I had read in the Bible. *No doubt!* The Bible is *not* a fairy-tale book. A few times, I actually felt Jesus walking behind me or beside me. I even turned around to look.

I knew I was on my way to digging deeper because there was so much more. It seemed the more I found out, the less confused I became. And guess what? It is not the Bible that is confusing, it is the way we read the Bible that makes it confusing. The Bible is not a book you just read and then put on the shelf.

Now we are going to skip up to the year 2013 when I moved to Florida. Almost right away, I joined a ladies' Bible study. It was a blessing to have a Messianic Jew as my teacher and leader. She had so much more knowledge about how the Old Testament and the New Testament fit together. I learned more from her in such a short period of time than I had in all my past about how the Old and New Testament connect. At the same time, I attended Mosaic Church in Winter Garden, Florida, a non-denominational church. I still couldn't believe how much I learned from Pastor Renaut van der Riet. He taught the Bible by making it come to life. He taught deep but with clarity, understanding, and application. Moving to Florida was definitely a God-thing. For five years, I was learning and studying from many different Bible studies and books of the Bible.

Then I moved to Indiana because that is where my husband's job is. But thanks to technology, I still watched and learned from the sermons by Pastor Renaut at Mosaic Church. Even before we got settled down in Indiana, I was searching for a Bible study group and a church where I could continue to learn from God's word and be around others who are also hungry to know God better. I attended a Tuesday morning ladies' bible study group every week (as life permits). Then on Wednesday evenings, with younger ladies, we had a group that grew out of a program called *Rooted*, from The Creek, a non-denominational church where we get together to share and strengthen our Christian walk with each other. Some of the ladies still brought and used the blessed gift of the printed bible.

There is no doubt that with all of these experiences, I learned more about how to understand the Bible, how we got the Bible, the history of the Bible, who wrote the Bible, and what the Bible is about.

I truly felt God kept tugging at heart, soul, and mind to write a book that will inspire more people to read the Bible after they have read this book. I honestly and prayerfully felt that it will clear up some of the confusion for you as well. This book is not just about me and my Christian walk but how the Bible has affected my life and how it could do that for you also. I just wanted to share my background and how God inspired me to write this book. I wanted to write in the simplest terms possible so that you too can start your journey into the Bible, and not be as confused, be afraid, or have doubt.

I cannot promise you will never be confused again or some things may not be as clear even after years of reading and studying the Scriptures.

This is a great way for me to share with you that you too can read the Bible and enjoy it with much less confusion. I was learning how to apply to my daily life what God tells me, even when things didn't feel so clear. No, I wasn't perfect. And many times throughout my life, I felt and still feel so many years were wasted doing what Sharon wanted to do, instead of following what God wanted me to do. Get to know God. His instructions are in his word, the Holy Bible. Just read it.

FUN FACTS: WHO, WHAT, HOW, AND DID YOU KNOW?

L et's start with some *fun facts.*

Who Wrote the Bible?

The Bible was not written by man's own interpretation.

God

God used about forty different writers over a period of approximately 1,500–1,600 years. Can you believe this! No other book in history could make this claim.

God was the ultimate author of the Bible from the beginning to end. God chose people from all walks of life to write down what He spiritually inspired and what He wanted us to know. "All scripture is given by inspiration of God, and is profitable for doctrine, for reproof, for correction, for instruction in righteousness" (2 Timothy 3:16 KJV).

People

The books of the bible were written down by shepherds, kings, construction workers, musicians, tax collectors, fishermen, physician, tent-makers, poets, songwriters, government officials, military leader, man comparable to an attorney at law, teenager, and priests. Which one can you relate to?

Scribes

Manuscripts were handwritten by Jewish scribes who had developed a very intricate and precise method of counting words and letters to ensure accuracy. Each word had to be said aloud as written. It had to be reviewed within thirty days. If up to three pages required corrections, the entire manuscript had to be re-written. Letters could not touch each other. The documents had to be stored in sacred places. No document containing God's Word could be destroyed. All were stored or buried. Only the writings that could be verified by the first recipient was copied by hand and then sent out to other Christ followers or churches. These writings were treated as sacred teachings.

Most of the New Testament writers knew Jesus personally. The other few writers were in a close relationship with the people who did know Jesus and was able to record firsthand accounts. And then there were those who had a personal spiritual encounter with Jesus.

What Is the Bible?

The Bible is one big book made up of sixty-six books.
The Old Testament consists of thirty-nine books.
The New Testament has twenty-seven books.
While some of the books are real-life stories, you will also find books about history, poems, law, psalms (songs), gospels, prophecy, and epistles (letters).

Who is the Bible about?

God. God is our Father in heaven. God is Jesus Christ in human form. God is the Holy Spirit in spiritual form.

How Was the Bible Written?

The Bible was not written in English. In fact, the English language didn't even exist when the Bible was first written.

The Bible was originally written in Hebrew, Aramaic, and Greek. It was later translated into numerous different languages.

The Old Testament was written in Hebrew with some Aramaic. The New Testament was written in Greek.

Did you know?

The first words of the Bible are "In the beginning…" (Genesis 1:1 ESV).

The last word of the Bible is "…Amen" (Revelation 22:21 NKJV).

BC means before the birth of Christ. The letters AD are Latin for Anno Domini, which means the year of our Lord Jesus Christ. AD does not mean *after death*.

BC and AD are used to number years in the calendar. The birth of Jesus Christ divided history and basically divides the OT from the NT.

Did you know? Prior to the Day of Pentecost, God provided the Holy Spirit to be *with* His believers, and at certain appointed times, the Holy Spirit was *in* the believer. Read Old Testament Micah 3:8 in any version. When Jesus was preparing the disciples for His ascension to heaven, He told them in John 14:26 (English Standard Version), "But the Helper, the Holy Spirit, whom the Father will send in my name, he will teach you all things and bring to your remembrance all that I have said."

Did you know? The Holy Spirit is part of the complete Trinity: The Father (God), Son (Jesus Christ), and Holy Spirit. You cannot have one without the other.

Did you know you can speak directly to the author of the Bible? God is the author. Because we pray through our Lord Jesus Christ, we have a direct line to the author.

Did you know? There is more than enough evidence to support what is written in the Bible. And there is more than enough evidence to prove the most recent translation is remarkably true to the original.

Did you know? The red letters in some Bible versions are the words that were spoken by Jesus Christ. Red letter editions were first used around 1899 highlighting the words that Jesus spoke because quotation marks were not present during that period of time.

Common Myths About the Bible

Did you know? Many sayings that have been around for many years or handed down from generations that are believed to be in the Bible are not actually written in the Bible and are not scriptural, which may be a cause for confusion. Here are just a few:

Money is the root of all evil. It is not. Read 1 Timothy 6:10 (New King James Version), "For the love of money is a root of all kinds of evil, for which some have strayed from the faith in their greediness, and pierced themselves through many sorrows."

Mary Magdalene was a prostitute. She was not. Read Luke 8:2 (New International Version) "And also some women who had been healed of evil spirits and diseases: Mary (called Magdalene) from whom seven demons had come out." She was one of Jesus's earliest followers, among other women, along with the disciples. Magdalene meaning a place called Magdala.

The Bible supports slavery (as we know it). It does not (but slavery did exist). There are many verses in the Bible that clear up these misunderstood statements or beliefs about slavery. God gave particular instructions on how to treat people that were in the role of being a servant.

See Definitions and Descriptions for the definition of the term slave as used in the Bible.

Old Testament—Exodus 21:16, Deuteronomy 15:12–18, 16:11–12

New Testament—Ephesians 6:9, Colossians 4:1

I recommend reading the full chapters of Exodus 21, Deuteronomy 15 and 16, also the full chapters of Ephesians 6 and Colossians 4 to understand slavery in the Bible and how God feels about it.

"*God will not give you more than you can handle.*" The Bible does not say that. To fully understand the meaning, you should read 1 Corinthians 10:13 (ERV), "The only temptations that you have are the same temptations that all people have. But you can trust God. He will not let you be tempted more than you can bear. But when you are tempted, God will also give you a way to escape that temptation. Then you will be able to endure it." In this verse, the Apostle Paul was referring to the temptation of sin, not that of sickness or trials of life. God *will* allow us more than we can humanly handle so that we will turn to him and stop relying on ourselves. Read 1 Corinthians chapter 10 and 2 Corinthians 1:8–9.

"*The devil made me do it.*" He does not. Let's blame Satan for our bad choices. The truth is, Satan will try to tempt us but we have to decide. "On reaching the place, he said to them, 'Pray that you will not fall into temptation'" (Luke 22:40 NIV). "But each person is tempted when they are dragged away by their own evil desires and enticed" (James 1:14 NIV).

Did any of these *Fun Facts* and *Did you know* tips help you understand more about the Bible?

Did you find answers to some of your questions in the facts listed above?

Did you read anything new that you did not know before?

Did you have any *ah-ha* moments?

HELPFUL HINTS: TIPS TO KNOW BEFORE READING THE BIBLE THAT WILL MAKE IT EASIER TO UNDERSTAND

Hint #1 Look at the Bible as God's bibliography, the big story about him. His true story from the beginning to the end with lots of real-life stories in between.

Hint #2 You don't need to know *everything* about the Bible or what is written in the Scriptures to become a Christian. Learning the Bible can be will be a lifelong journey. I personally know a lady in her nineties who has been reading the Bible since she was a child. She told me she is still learning.

Hint #3 It is very important to remember you cannot change the meaning of what the author meant.

Hint #4 Be very careful not to take words, phrases, and Scriptures out of context. See the chapter *Taken Out of Context! What Does that Mean?*

Hint #5 How to understand what the numbers mean that are in front of or behind the name of the books of the Bible. For example, Genesis 3:1–19. Genesis is the name of the book. The 3 is the chapter. The 1–19 means verse 1 through verse 19. Here is another example, 1 Peter 2:1. The 1 in front of the name Peter is the first book of Peter because Peter wrote two books. 1 Peter is the first book of Peter, chapter 2 verse 1.

Hint #6 When you are reading the Bible, do not spend too much time with the pronunciation or how to say a particular word. As long as the way you say it does not change the meaning, just do the best you can. There are websites on the internet and apps that you can put on your phone that you can access if you want to hear how words are pronounced. When you are in a classroom setting or even by yourself and you come to a word that seems to have every letter in the alphabet and you know you would mess it up when you try to read it, don't fret, just do the best you can and go on. Unless you know the Hebrew, Aramaic, or Greek language, you will probably not say the words as originally spoken in those languages anyway.

Hint #7 Try to put aside any preconceived ideas or training that you grew up with until you read this book, and then read the Bible with a new outlook. Just because we were taught something and it became a ritual or man-made practice, does not mean it's in the Bible. This is just a suggestion because I had to do the same thing, and it truly helped.

Hint #8 It's never too late to start reading your own Bible. The Bible can be confusing because you may not have been taught the Bible when you were growing up, whether you attended church or not. Some churches or denominations do not teach the Bible, or they may have taught just certain sections or books of the Bible.

Hint #9 You can start in the New Testament and read the four Gospels (Gospel means Good News) first. Matthew, Mark, Luke, and John each wrote about their own personal experiences or from eyewitness accounts concerning the birth, life, ministry, death, and resurrection of Jesus Christ. Or you can start in the book of Genesis, which is the first book of the Bible and read through to the end of the book of Revelation.

Hint #10 Do not try to read the Book of Revelation as your first choice! Talk about confusion.

Hint #11 Try not to assume what you think is in the Bible, or don't rely on what someone else has told you unless you know it is in the Bible. That can result in confusion.

Hint #12 Pay special attention to when you hear the wording *interpretation vs. translation*. Look up these two words in the Definitions and Descriptions section.

Hint #13 When reading the Bible, whatever version, you need to keep in mind the time period in which it was written.

Hint #14 To help you find the different books in the Bible, it is a good idea to add tabs to each book. Some Bibles come with pre-tabbed pages to help find the book of the Bible much easier.

Hint #15 Be careful what you read about Scripture and what source you are reading it from. Verify the information from reliable sources. Do not believe everything you read until you check it out in the Bible for yourself.

Hint #16 The Bible is not bound and printed in chronological order, but there are study books that are prepared and printed in date order in which the books were written. Those Bibles are called Chronological Study Bibles.

CHAPTER 1

HOW DID WE GET THE BIBLE? FROM STONE TO PAPER

Materials used to write the Scripture

It is interesting to know that people have been using various types of material to communicate and record information for many centuries. Evidence of writings has been found dating back to 2700 BC. In addition to stone, clay, leather, parchment, and vellum and before the use of paper, other materials such as wax-covered wood tablets were also found.

Stone

Ancient Scriptures, as recorded in the Old Testament, were etched in stone. God used stone to write the law and commandments. "The Lord said to Moses, 'Come up to me on the mountain and stay here, and I will give you the tablets of *stone* with the law and commandments I have written for their instructions" (Exodus 24:12 NIV). As you see, God was the first one to invent *tablets*, and He didn't even need a battery or electricity. His tablet was also a *touch screen*. God wrote the commandments on the stone tablets using His finger. Here are a few more verses that talk about stone being used for writing on: Exodus 31:18, 32:15–16, 34:1; Deuteronomy 5:22; and Joshua 8:31–32.

Clay

In the book of Ezekiel, you will see clay was used to draw a map of Jerusalem (Ezekiel 4:1).

Leather

Leather was thick, dense, and not flexible. It was not easy to write on. However, history shows the use of leather to write on lasted about four thousand years.

Papyrus

Papyrus was made from stalks of a reed plant grown in Egypt along the Nile. The plant was pressed to make sheets and could be attached together to form scrolls and then could be written on. Carbon-based ink made from soot, gum, and water was used with a reed-type pen. Papyrus was used for writing material approximately three thousand years.

> Having many things to write unto you, I would not write with paper and ink: but I trust to come unto you, and speak face to face, that our joy may be full. (2 John 12 KJV)

Parchment or Vellum

Parchment, vellum, and leather were created from fine animal skins. Parchment was a general term for the animal skins that were prepared for writing. Parchment made from calfskin was called vellum.

Paper

The first Bible to be printed on paper was in 1455 on the Gutenberg Printing Press. According to *Guinness World Records*, the Bible is the world's best-selling and most widely distributed book. The most recent estimates shows the number of printed copies well over five billion.

SO YOU THINK THE BIBLE IS CONFUSING

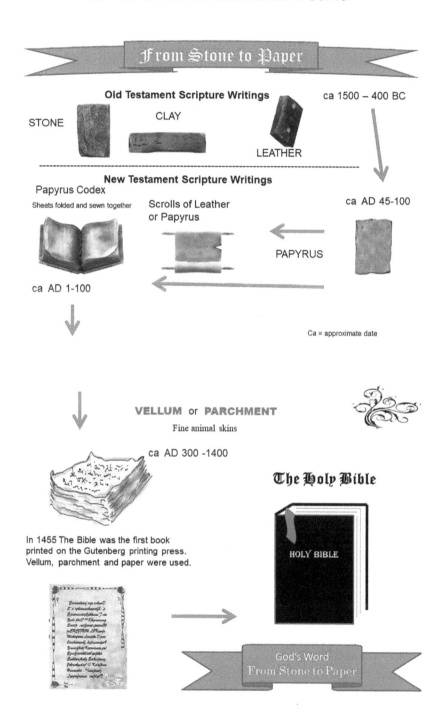

From Stone to Paper

Old Testament Scripture Writings ca 1500 – 400 BC

STONE

CLAY

LEATHER

New Testament Scripture Writings

Papyrus Codex

Sheets folded and sewn together

Scrolls of Leather or Papyrus

ca AD 45-100

PAPYRUS

ca AD 1-100

Ca = approximate date

VELLUM or **PARCHMENT**

Fine animal skins

ca AD 300 -1400

The Holy Bible

In 1455 The Bible was the first book printed on the Gutenberg printing press. Vellum, parchment and paper were used.

HOLY BIBLE

God's Word
From Stone to Paper

CHAPTER 2

WHEN WAS THE BIBLE WRITTEN?

Have you ever wondered how in the world did all of these books of the Bible come together and when were they written? The books did not just fall out of the sky to form the Bible. Most biblical scholars agreed that the first writings of the Bible dated back to 1450 BC. That was 1,450 years before the birth of Jesus Christ. According to archeological findings, historical research, documented witnesses, and from the words of Moses himself, we could trust that the writings of the first five books (sometimes called the Pentateuch) were written by Moses as inspired by God. The Book of Job might have been written before or during that time period as well. The Old Testament is a combination of the thirty-nine books written over a period of one thousand years, from 1450 BC to 425 BC. Now isn't that amazing and miraculous (1,450 years before and up to 425 years prior to Jesus's birth).

During the time period between 425 BC and AD 45, other books were written but were not universally accepted by the majority of all the different religious leaders, or they were rejected according to the strict standards set by the canon. The canon was the criteria that had to be met in order for the books to be included in the Bible. The New Testament consisted of the twenty-seven books that were written from about AD 45 to AD 95, with the last book being the book of Revelation which was written by the Apostle John as inspired by God. According to the Gospels of Luke, John, and Mark, the approximate date that Jesus was crucified was about AD 33, so it was only twelve years later that the first books of the New Testament were beginning to be written.

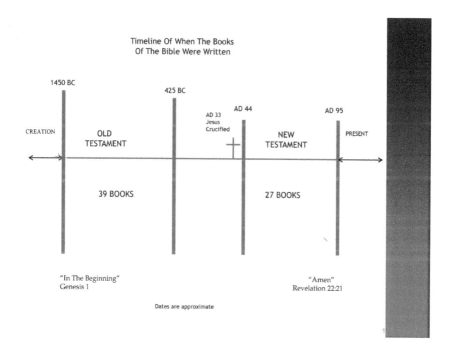

Timeline Of When The Books
Of The Bible Were Written

1450 BC

425 BC

AD 33
Jesus
Crucified

AD 44

AD 95

CREATION

OLD
TESTAMENT

NEW
TESTAMENT

PRESENT

39 BOOKS

27 BOOKS

"In The Beginning"
Genesis 1

"Amen"
Revelation 22:21

Dates are approximate

CHAPTER 3

WHICH VERSION OF THE BIBLE SHOULD I READ?

Well, first, what do you mean by the word *version*? What is a version?

"A particular form of something that is slightly different from other forms of the same thing" (Cambridge Dictionary, 2017). A version does not mean a different language.

Here is a simple way to look at it: Take three eggs. Open one egg to make a scrambled egg, take the second egg and fry it, and then put the third egg in a pot to boil. We have three different versions of an egg, but it's still an egg. Like three different versions of the Bible, it is still the Bible. Wasn't that fun?

So now you can ask: Which version or translation should I read? I personally cannot answer that question for you. What I can suggest, though, is to borrow, go online, or buy gently used Bible versions. A great resource is www.BibleGateway.com to read the different versions if you prefer electronics instead of printed Bibles.

You will want to view several different versions to see which one you are more comfortable with. On www.BibleGateway.com, you can view different versions at the same time, side by side. A good idea is to pick several verses or chapters from a Bible and then read that same verse or chapter in the different versions. From that, you may be able to determine which version you are more comfortable reading and understanding. I personally use the New Living Translation, the English Standard Version, the New International Version, and the Contemporary English Version for study and clarity. I do read and use others as well for comparison.

The King James Version was my first Bible, which I cherish for its poetic beauty and historic English language. Many people tell me the King James Version is confusing. That is probably because it was originally written in 1604–1611, during the same time period that William Shakespeare was writing in the language of that day (not the same English as today). Do you remember in school when you had to read Shakespeare for English class? Some students enjoyed it while others absolutely did not. Have you ever read *Romeo and Juliet*? It is considered to be a beautiful poetic language and is still used in the arts even today. Yet it is difficult to understand if you don't have an interest in that particular language style. I am not implying that you should not read or use the King James Bible—there are updated versions.

The King James Bible was the most popular version for about three hundred years. The most updated one is the twenty-first Century King James Version published in 1994. It is not a new translation. It was just edited to update the wording to the words that we use today, but it did not change the original meaning of the word. The editors were careful to keep the beautiful language while making it easier to read and understand.

Who was King James? See Definitions and Descriptions. Did you know how the King James Bible came to be? Read on. According to *The World's Greatest Book:*

> Due to the religious friction among the different churches, King James wanted to bring some peace and unity to the people. There were many bibles already in circulation when King James ordered fifty-four highly intelligent, very respected and handpicked scholars to write a new bible. The writers were told and encouraged to refer to and use other English translations but demanded the new bible be for all

people, and contain only biblical text leaving out all other notes that caused the people to be divided. With great precision and accuracy, after seven long years, the King James Bible was completed in 1611 (Lawrence H. Schiffman, PhD, Jerry Pattengale, PhD. *The World's Greatest Book.* (Worthy Publishing, 2017), 204–209).

The written Scriptures dated back to approximately one thousand five hundred BC, so we will not cover all of the different versions (translations) that were in circulation over that long period of time.

The Bible was the first book to be printed in Latin on the Gutenberg printing press in AD 1455. The printing press technology allowed for mass production, publishing, and mass distribution of the Bible.

Below is a list of fourteen different English versions (translations) of the Bible and when they were printed. Keep in mind, translating is not interpreting. Translation does not change the meaning; however, interpreting can change the meaning to the person who is doing the interpreting. There were also numerous translations between the year 1535 and 1604 that is not included.

The list contains fourteen different versions of the many that are available today. Realistically, I don't think anyone is going to try to read from all of the versions just to be able to choose which two or three they are most comfortable with and make sense to them.

1. 1535: The first complete Bible to be printed in the English language (not American English) was the Cloverdale Bible in the year 1535. The Bible was already in circulation before the King James Version was printed.
2. 1604: AKJV—The translation of the Authorized King James Version, which is also referred to as the King James Version, was originally started in 1604, written and published in 1611 in the Old English language.

3. 1870: KJV—Scholars in England made revisions to the 1611 King James Bible to reflect the information found in the manuscripts of the ancient Hebrew.
4. 1885: ERV—The English Revised Version was a British revision of King James.
5. 1901: ASV (American Standard Version) was the revision from King James English into American English.
6. 1978: NIV (New International Version) was readable-easy to understand.
7. 1982: NKJV (New King James Version) was modernized King James Version.
8. 1989: ERV (Easy-to-Read Version) was created for new readers, simple vocabulary and shorter sentences.
9. 1991: CEV (Contemporary English Version) was natural uncomplicated English.
10. 1995: NASB (New American Standard Bible) was accurate and readable word-for-word translation.
11. 1996: NLT (New Living Translation) was the revision of the Living Bible.
12. 2001: ESV (English Standard Version) was the literal update of the Revised Standard Version.
13. 2005: NET (New English Translation) was the complete translation of the original biblical languages into English
14. 2019: NET (New English Translation) was the newest edition with major updates.

For an additional list of versions or translations of the Bible see: *The Rose Book of Bible Charts, Maps and Time Lines* and BibleGateway. com

Here is a true story, food for thought when trying to decide where to start, which one to pick first when trying to find one that is easy to read if you are a beginner and new to reading a Bible. My dear friend, Pam, and I went shopping at a Half Price Book store searching for a Bible that her husband could easily read and understand. He had received a serious brain injury as a result of an accident on a construction site. We both searched through various versions and she chose the Easy to Read Version (ERV). It *is* easy to read. I bought the New International Version (NIV) StoryLine Bible to share with my family.

The Storyline Bible was written like a continuous story, simple, easy to read and understand. It was written for adults, not children. It was written in English for today, not in the Shakespearian-type language. Just like a storybook, it provided maps, graphs, illustrations, and pictures, and each chapter has a description and summary of what the chapter is about. Keep in mind, I am not promoting one version over the other. You may find you like a different one.

Exercise:

You may or may not have any Bibles in front of you right now, but when you do, get at least two different versions, come back to this chapter, and practice the fun exercises below. The goal is to get you to see that the versions say the same thing and they just use different wording.

You will need to get access to two or three different versions of the Bible and then look up the verses listed below. You will see that there are two verses from the Old Testament and two verses from the New Testament. For this little exercise, we want to focus our attention on how each version of the Bible uses different words but have the same meaning. Remember, all translations come from the original languages of Hebrew, Aramaic, or Greek.

Here is a little guide on how to look up books, chapters, and versions in the Bible.

Example: Genesis 1:1. Genesis is the first book of the Bible in the Old Testament. The *1* is the first chapter, and then the next *1* is the first verse.

1. *New International Version* (NIV): Genesis 1:1 *In the beginning God made the heaven and the earth.*
2. *Easy-to-Read Version* (ERV): Genesis 1:1 *God created the sky and the earth. At first.*
3. *New King James Version* (NKJV): Genesis 1:1 *In the beginning God created the heavens and the earth.*

If you have three versions, then write all three to compare.

Example: Psalm 23:1–3. Psalm is the book of Psalms, the nineteenth book about halfway through the Old Testament, chapter 23, verses 1 through 3. You may need to use additional paper. Write the name of the version on the first blank line and then the verse on the second blank line.

1. _____ Version: Psalm 23:1–3 _____
2. _____ Version: Psalm 23:1–3 _____
3. _____ Version: Psalm 23:1–3 _____

Example: John 3:16, the book of John in the first part of the New Testament, the fourth book of the four Gospels (after Matthew, Mark, Luke), chapter 3, verse 16. Write the name of the version on the first blank line and then the verse on the second blank line.

1. _____ Version: John 3:16 _____
2. _____ Version: John 3:16 _____
3. _____ Version: John 3:16 _____

Example: Ephesians 2:8, the book of Ephesians, the tenth book in the New Testament, chapter 2, verse 8. Write the name of the version on the first blank line and then the verse on the second blank line.

1. _____ Version: Ephesians 2:8 _____
2. _____ Version: Ephesians 2:8 _____
3. _____ Version: Ephesians 2:8 _____

Which version was easier for you to read and understand?
_____

Note: You may also want to choose a few more books of the Bible and verses on your own to compare the different versions of the Bible. After you become comfortable with one or two, you will find that the Bible is not as confusing as you thought. The purpose of this chapter is to address one of the reasons people feel the Bible is confusing. Now that you have looked at the different versions, do you feel a little more relaxed and not so confused?

No matter what version or translation of the Bible you decide to read with all the little *differences,* the most important thing to remember is that overall, they all say the same thing. From Genesis to Revelation, our God is leading you to His son, Jesus Christ. Don't get hung up or confused by the versions. Decide on one or two, and get to reading.

CHAPTER 4

BIBLICAL TRANSLATION VS INTERPRETATION

We first need to know the definition or meaning of these two words. Let's start with translation. Biblical translation "is the art and practice of rendering the Bible into languages other than those in which it was originally written" (https://www.britannica.com/topic/biblical-translation).

Translation is used in written form.

Interpretation "is the act of explaining, reframing or showing your own understanding of something" (https://www.vocabulary.com/dictionary/interpretation).

Interpretation is used in spoken, verbal, or oral form.

These two words are not the same.

The original Scriptures were written in Hebrew, some Aramaic, and in the Greek language. Most of the Old Testament was written in Hebrew. In the later part of the Old Testament, some of the writing was in the Aramaic language. The Hebrew Scriptures were first *translated* into Greek.

The New Testament was *originally written* in Greek. During the period of the Roman Empire and the spread of the Christian faith, the Scriptures were *translated* from Greek into Latin. The Bible continued to be *translated* into multiple languages throughout the world. When the Scriptures were being *translated*, the writers were not changing the meaning or the context based on their own understanding. They were transferring from one language to another.

For example, let's say you are in a French class and for now you only know the English language. Your homework is to write in French what your paper shows in English. You will need to translate it correctly, or you will not get an *A*. The teacher is not going to allow for just an interpretation of what you think it means in French. You will need to translate the words from English into French.

I hope this helps you understand that we cannot change the meaning of what the author meant.

God is the author of the Bible. There will be many times we will come across verses that we will not understand. I have heard over and over *well that's how I interpreted it*. And it very well may be that God is revealing the true meaning to you. Some verses of the Scripture are difficult to understand if you don't read the full chapter or even the entire book of the Bible. The purpose of this chapter is to highlight when the different versions of the Bible were being translated from one language to another. They are not interpreted as some folks may believe.

CHAPTER 5

WHAT THE BIBLE IS. WHAT THE BIBLE IS NOT. SPOILER ALERT

H ave you ever had someone tell you about a book they just read? Did you feel like it was a *spoiler alert*. And it made you feel like you know all about it, and now you don't need to read it? Or did it make you want to hurry up and read it for yourself? Do you read books based on what others say about it, or do you choose what books you want to read? Do you ever start from the back of the book to find out the ending before you decide to read it or not? Maybe you are curious and look in the middle of the book. Do you like people telling you their opinion on the type of book it is or is not?

Some people *judge* a book by its cover. That is like deciding if a recipe is going to taste good just by the name of it. Or you know you will love it based on the colorful illustration even before eating it first. But then you find out after taking a few bites or even after eating the whole thing, the flavor was not what you expected. It did not taste like you thought it would based on the *title* of the recipe or the tempting photo.

Below is a list of *spoiler alerts* that give you an idea of what the *Bible is* and what the *Bible is not*. Read the Bible, and find out for yourself.

We are going to approach this chapter a little different. This is not a quiz. It's just a few thought-provoking suggestions. After you have written down your response, then read through this chapter to discover some thoughts and facts on what the Bible is and what the Bible is not. (Don't get bored. Hang in there, it's worth it.)

Take a few minutes and write down your own thoughts of what the Bible is.

_____

Now take a few minutes and write down what you think the Bible is not.

_____

If someone asked you, "What is the Bible?" How would you answer?

_____

The *Bible* is:

The greatest book ever written.

(That's not only my opinion but that of many people throughout history.)

The Bible is the best-selling book in the world (www.guinnesworldrecords.com, Aug 2, 2021).

The Bible is *the book.*

The Bible is Scripture, sacred writings.

The Old Testament is/was written in Hebrew, with some Aramaic.

The New Testament is/was written in Greek.

The Bible is one big recipe with four main ingredients: The creation, the fall, the redemption, and the restoration.

The Bible is God's story. It is a book about God.

The Bible is now translated into thousands of different languages.

The Bible is written in many languages that are available to us today.

The Bible is His one big book with sixty-six mini books that come together to create His big story.

The Bible is written by about forty different authors over a period of approximately one thousand five hundred years.

The Bible is a book whose ultimate author is God.

The Bible is a book that contains more than just true stories. You will find history, poems, law, psalms (songs), Gospels, more history, epistles (letters), and prophecy.

The Bible is organized with similar topics, subjects, or genres.

The Bible is true. The Dead Sea Scrolls prove the reliability of the original writings that has been found so far as research is still being performed.

The Bible is about how God created us, how He loves us, and how He forgives us not matter who we are or what we have done.

The Bible is God's instructions which still apply to us as much today as when it was written.

The Bible is about God's chosen people, the Jewish people as recorded in the Old Testament.

The Bible is about Christianity in the New Testament.

The Bible is two main books put together as one. That is the Old Testament and the New Testament.

The Bible is full of very important geography.

The Bible is full of science.

The Bible is God's words written for us, not to us.

The Bible is a book written for us to use and apply to our daily lives.

The Bible is a book with verses that will answer just about any topic, trial, tribulation, and challenge.

The Bible is a book that has answers to most who, what, when, where, and why questions.

The Bible is a combination of ancient songs, oral traditions, wise sayings, letters, decrees, historical records, and eyewitness test.

The Bible is full of history.

The Bible is a book full of real people, with real lives, personal stories, and experiences.

The Bible is a book of Scriptures that are better preserved than any other writings in history.

The Bible is for everyone.

The Bible is complete, closed. No one can add or subtract from the original scriptures. The Old Testament was completed with the book of Malachi approximately 425 BC. The New Testament was completed and final with the book of Revelation around AD 95.

The *Bible is not:*

The Bible is not just *A* book.

The Bible is not just another religious book.

The Bible is not a history book.

The Bible is not a geography book.

The Bible is/was not originally written in English.

The Bible is not written in chronological order.

The Bible is/was not written by man's own interpretation. "All scripture is inspired by God and is useful to teach us what is true and to make us realize what is wrong in our lives. It corrects us when we are wrong and teaches us to do what is right" (2 Timothy 3:16 NLT).

The Bible is not some ancient out-of-date instruction booklet.

The Bible is not interpreted by scholars to say what they wanted it to say but was translated word for word or thought for thought what the text said.

The Bible is not about denominations.

The Bible is not a book of contradiction.

The Bible is not sugar-coated to make us *feel* good.

The Bible is not a book of fairy tales, bedtime stories, or a storybook about fictional characters.

The Bible is not a science book.

The Bible is not just for religious people.

Did you find that you already knew some of the facts, thoughts, or ideas as the ones listed above?

CHAPTER 6

WHERE IS IT? HOW TO FIND A PARTICULAR BOOK IN THE BIBLE

The Bible was not printed in chronological order, meaning it was not put together as a book in the date order in which the events happened or when the book was originally written. The Bible was arranged in genres, which means types of categories.

Take a look at the illustrations below, *Books of the Bible Library*, which represents the Old Testament and the New Testament. The books were in order starting from left to right and top to bottom if the books are stacked.

How many times have you been in church, a Bible study, watching a sermon from home, or just wanting to find a certain book of the Bible but didn't know where to start? Before technology, like cell phones, smartphones, tablets, and so on, finding a particular verse was a challenge. Like myself and many other folks, you have your printed Bible when you are sitting in church listening to the pastor, preacher, teacher, or whoever, and they say, "Okay, everyone, if you have your Bible, let's turn to the book of Psalms and look at Psalm chapter 9 verse 1."

Yikes, where is the book of Psalms? You started flipping pages. You didn't know where to start—in the back, in the front. Look in the middle. By the time you finally find it, probably because you elbowed the person next to you to help or you hurried to the index, the Pastor has passed that verse and went on to something else. I certainly have played that tune over and over. Please do not get too overwhelmed, feel inferior, or give up. It takes time to get comfortable with knowing where the books are in the Bible.

There isn't any real easy way to know all of the books right away unless you are blessed with the gift of memorizing where all sixty-six books are. You may be good at it. I never was. Even in Sunday school the only verse I really could remember is John 3:16, which I knew was a book in the New Testament. No credit here, I think believers and non-believers alike know that one.

Let me help you make this a little easier. The books in Bible were not in alphabetical order. However, most bibles printed today do have an alphabetical index.

The first thing you need to know is there are two main sections, the Old Testament and the New Testament. The OT is first section.

The second step is to know that the OT has thirty-nine books, and the NT has twenty-seven books for a total of sixty-six books.

The third step is to write down the name of the first five or six books in order, starting with Genesis. Practice reading the names of those that you wrote down until you are comfortable, and then add five or six more of the next books. Continue with this practice until you are at the end of the Bible. You don't necessarily need to memorize the books in order. This just gives you a basic sense of where they are.

You may also want to tab each book. Some Bibles are already tabbed, so when you are shopping for a Bible, look for the ones that are tabbed. Now I know this may sound like a lot of time and trouble, but it will be worth it when you see what you have accomplished. If you are reading this book, which I know you are, to show my appreciation, I will send you a *free* bookmark with the lists of all the sixty-six books. Then you can have it with you to refer to quickly. Please email your request to: sharonrkenner17@gmail.com. (Don't forget the *r* in the middle.) Include your name, mailing address, and where you got your copy of this book.

Or

The easy way to look up books, chapters, and verses is to use your electronic device. You may not be able to memorize all the books, but again you may not need to when using an app. You can add an app like BibleGateway.com or any other that you may find you are comfortable with. I personally like Bible Gateway because you can choose one version or view a couple at the same time for comparison. It also provides a search box where you just type in the book, chapter, and verse that you need in an instant. So now when the pastor asks you to go to the book of Psalms chapter 9:1, you can quickly get there. No more flipping pages, fanning through in frustration, or elbowing the person next to you.

I personally cherish my printed Bibles and will continue to use them for reading at home or using in a Bible study setting so I can make notes. I do find it easier though in church or at home to use my device with the app to keep up with the live sermon. These days you can watch recorded sermons and hit the pause button when you need to look up the verse. Now isn't that a blessing? However, electronic devices and technology will never substitute the experience of attending church in person.

I hope this helps you get a little more comfortable with finding a book in the Bible. It may be easier than you thought.

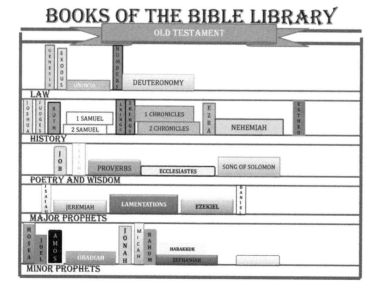

BOOKS OF THE BIBLE LIBRARY

NEW TESTAMENT

MATTHEW				JOHN
	MARK	LUKE		

GOSPELS

ACTS

HISTORY

ROMANS				
	1CORINTHIANS	GALATIANS	PHILIPPIANS	1 THESSALONIANS
	2CORINTHIANS	EPHESIANS	COLOSSIANS	2 THESSALONIANS

EPISTLES (letters) TO CHURCHES

1 TIMOTHY		
2 TIMOTHY	TITUS	PHILEMON

EPISTLES (letters) TO FRIENDS

JAMES		1 JOHN	JUDE
	1 PETER	2 JOHN	
HEBREWS	2 PETER	3 JOHN	REVELATION

GENERAL (letters) EPISTLES

CHAPTER 7

HOW DO I KNOW THE BIBLE IS TRUE?

I truly believe most people want to know that the Bible is true. They may have doubts because they have heard critics and others who really just have not even read the Bible or those who don't believe in it say that it is not true. Most people who do not believe the Bible is true base their opinion on what they have heard, not what they know. That goes hand in hand with being confused. On one hand, you want to believe the Bible is true, but on the other hand, you are not sure. So that could cause confusion.

There are more reasons to believe the Bible is true than the few reasons not to believe it's true. I listed the top few reasons that I hear the most from people of why they question the Bible and its truthfulness. With upward of twenty thousand surviving copies, some within twenty years of the originals, the books of the New Testament have the greatest manuscript support of any document from ancient history. Even non-Christian scholars attest to the fact that the Bible is the best-preserved literary work surviving from antiquity.

Does the Bible contradict itself?

Have you ever heard that the Bible is full of contradictions? Some of the perceived *contradictions* are from within the Bible and others are what people *think* the Bible says instead of what it actually says.

First let us look at the word *contradiction* to find out what it means to contradict.

1. A situation or ideas in opposition to one another (www. vocabulary.com/dictionary/contradiction).
2. A proposition, statement, or phrase that implies both the truth and falsity of something (www.merriam-webster. com).
3. To contradict—deny the truth of a statement by asserting the opposite (Oxford English Dictionary).
4. The fact of something being the complete opposite of something else or very different from something else, so that one of them must be wrong (Cambridge Dictionary).

Here is a common scenario: You and a friend went to an event together. You had fun. You ate a hot dog, but your friend had nachos. You came across someone you knew, but your friend had walked away for a few minutes so he didn't meet that person. It was sunny for a while, but then it started to rain. After you returned home, you told your family about your experience. You told them the food was not really that good. Your friend was saying the food was great. You mentioned that you ran into an old buddy. Your friend said he didn't see anyone he knew. You were telling them how it was nice and sunny. But your friend was saying how you guys got rained on.

So you see how the same event, experienced by two different people, seemed contradictory, but it wasn't.

#1 There are verses within the Bible that contradict other verses. This common misunderstanding is easy to explain. It falls back to needing to read the verse in context, which means you need to read the full verse or chapter from beginning to end to understand the place, the time, the situation, and who the author was talking to and the event they were talking about.

Example: Same writer, same time, same scenario:
"And of every living thing of all flesh, you shall bring two of every sort into the ark to keep them alive with you" (Genesis 6:19 ESV).

"Take with you seven pairs of all clean animals, the male and his mate, and a pair of the animals that are not clean, the male and his mate" (Genesis 7:2 ESV).

Not a contradiction. God told Noah in verse 6:19, two of every sort that did not change in verse 7:2. God went on to specify in detail seven pairs (a pair is still two) of all clean animals. That command did not change or take away the fact that it still fell within the *two of every sort*.

Side note: If you really want to know more about Noah, the ark, and the animals, visit The Ark Encounter located in Williamstown, Kentucky. It is definitely worth the travel (https://arkencounter.com).

Example: Two different writers, same scenario:

"And after six days Jesus took with him Peter and James and John his brother, and led them up a high mountain by themselves" (Matthew 17:1 ESV).

"Now about eight days after these sayings he took with him Peter and John and James and went up on the mountain to pray" (Luke 9:28 ESV).

The verses are about the promise and the transfiguration. Matthew is referring to the six days in-between the day Jesus made the promise and the day of His transfiguration. As stated, Luke said *about* which was not an exact day. He included the day of the promise and the day of the transfiguration. This would add up to eight days. So this is not a contradiction as critics want to accuse.

In some instances, two verses from two different writers seem to say the opposite concerning the same thing, but after further reading, you'll find the statements were different, not contradictory.

Also it is very important to understand that the Bible was written in Hebrew, Aramaic, and Greek.

Was the Bible written by humans?

Yes, the Bible was penned by humans. Every book ever written was penned by humans, including all text books that we use in schools, colleges, universities, the workplace, and for pleasure. Do we trust those books because they were written by humans? All the knowledge we have was and is written by humans. There are numerous books that are written but have changed over the years or the information was updated to reflect current reality. The Bible has not changed. Most history books do not change unless findings that have been made influence that change. The discoveries by archeologist have not changed what is written in the Bible, but in fact they have confirmed what is in the Bible.

How could we as humans relate to a *book* if it was just zapped into existence from a supernatural source? Of course, our one and only God has the power to do that, but what would be the purpose? Our perfect God used imperfect humans to relate to imperfect humans to tell us His perfect message.

Of course, humans make errors. God does not make errors. An error is not an error until it is found to be an error by verifiable sources. The writers/humans whom God used were normal everyday people. Miraculously, these people wrote what God inspired them to write. No human, in his limited wisdom and knowledge, would ever be capable of writing what we have in the Bible and to be consistent throughout the ages. Other religions have been found to *update* or make changes to their *religious book* to fit or adhere to the culture of the day. The Holy Bible has not changed.

The Bible was written by forty different people approximately over one thousand five hundred years. See: resources such as answersingenesis.org, Christianity.org, *How do We Know the Bible is True* by Ken Ham and Bodie Hodge, just to name a few. There exist multiple sources that agree on the number of writers and the time span in which the books were written. Also check out the book *Evidence That Demands a Verdict* by Josh McDowell. This is nothing less than miraculous and more than just a *God wink*.

Here are just a few reasons you Can believe the Bible is true.

#1 It is historically accurate.

Authentic archeological finds confirm our biblical text. See these resources:

1. https://www.crossway.org/articles/10-crucial-archaeological-discoveries-related-to-the-bible/
2. https://answersingenesis.org/archaeology/
3. 100 Proofs for the Bible Old Testament found in *Rose Book of Bible Charts, Maps and Time Line*

#2 Prophecy has been fulfilled.

What is a prophecy? It is a message from God concerning the past, present, and future. A prophecy is not just a prediction about the future.

You can find in the Old Testament and into the New Testament events and happenings that were told of things to come, did come, and will continue to come. But God warns us about false prophets. *Well then what is a prophet? A prophet is a person chosen by God to speak his message. So what is a false prophet? It is anyone who self-claims to speak God's message but was not chosen by God.* They are from the world; therefore, they speak from the world, and the world listens to them. Just because people claim to be a prophet, that doesn't mean they are. I am sure you have heard about the big bad wolf in the story of *Little Red Riding Hood.* The wolf was dressed in sweet little granny's clothing to fool the little innocent girl. You need to heed to God's warning, know the Scriptures, or you too will be fooled by the wolf.

The prophets named in the Bible were chosen by God.

> Beware of false prophets, which come to you in sheep's clothing, but inwardly they are raving wolves…Wherefore by their fruits ye shall know them. (Matthew 7:15–20 KJV)

Beloved, do not believe every spirit, but test the spirits to see whether they are from God, for many false prophets have gone out into the world. By this you know the Spirit of God: every spirit that confesses that Jesus Christ has come in the flesh is from God, and every spirit that does not confess Jesus is not from God. This is the spirit of the antichrist, which you heard was coming and now is in the world already. (1 John 4:1–3 ESV)

You can trust the prophecies told about in the Bible, because they did come true. Most of them were written many, many years before the event actually happened. Miraculously! Some prophetic messages in the book of Revelation are yet to come.

#3 Scientific accuracy
Astronomy: Stars are innumerable (Genesis 22:17).
Geology: Water cycle (Ecclesiastes 1:7), sea currents (Psalms 8:8).
Biology: Blood circulation (Leviticus 17:11).
Anthropology: All humans are one blood (Genesis 3:20, Acts 17:26, 1 Corinthians 15:45
answersingenesis.org).

#4 Amazing preservation
"The evidence for our New Testament writings is ever so much greater than the evidence for many writings of classical authors, the authenticity of which no one dreams of questioning. The accumulation of manuscript evidence has been so vast and the work of the scientific textual critic so precise that we may express complete confidence in the reliability of the New Testament text. Let me emphasize how impressive this fact really is.

The New Testament documents have been in existence almost nineteen hundred years. For fifteen of these centuries they were replicated solely by hand. In spite of this, there are only some twelve to twenty **significant** textual variations in the entire New Testament, and none of these affect an important doctrinal matter. On the other hand, consider the works of William Shakespeare. These writings have existed less than four centuries (and since the invention of the printing press) and yet: We can only stand in awe of the providential preservation of the sacred text of the word of God. We can trust the Bible. It is a book by which we can both live and die" (https://www.christiancourier.com/articles/1441-the-new-testament-compared-to-classical-literature. Jackson, Wayne. "The New Testament Compared to Classical literature." *ChristianCourier.com*. Access date: August 13, 2021).

#5 Lives Changed

The impact that the Bible has had on individual lives as well as all societies around the world and throughout history speaks for itself as being truthful. There are numerous well known and famous people that originally had claimed to be atheist but converted to some form of Christianity (https://en.wikipedia.org/wiki/List_of_converts_to_Christianity_from_nontheism)

Kirk Cameron: actor, evangelist, and TV show host

Lee Strobel: award-winning legal editor, best-selling author (book turned movie *God's not Dead* series), apologist, and speaker (https://leestrobel.com/about).

C. S. Lewis: writer, scholar, theologian, Christian apologetic, and author of the well-known series *Chronicles of Narnia* (https://christianity.org.uk/article/cs-lewis).

Leah Libresco: writer, school systems analyst, speaker, and former atheist blogger (http://www.leahlibresco.com/)

#6 Jesus Christ used Scripture

Jesus referred to and used the Hebrew scripture during His earthly ministry. If Jesus Christ trusted the Scriptures to be true, then why shouldn't we? Here are a few that you can look up: In Matthew 4:4, Jesus quoted Deuteronomy 8:3. In Matthew 15:7–9, He referred to Isaiah 29:13, and in Mark 10:7–8, He quoted Genesis 2:24. Jesus's lifetime and ministry was during the period of the New

Testament when He is teaching God's word from the Old Testament. If for no other reason to trust the Bible, Jesus trusts the Scriptures, and so should you.

The most profound and no-excuse reason for believing that the Bible is true: *God is the author.*

CHAPTER 8

HOW THE BIBLE IS MISREPRESENTED: *CHRISTIAN* BEHAVIOR THAT MISREPRESENTS THE BIBLE

This can be confusing.

I agree, why would anyone want to read or trust the Bible or any book for that matter, if the teachings that it produces is hatred against certain people, money hungry dishonest televangelists, holier-than-thou or *holy rollers*, hypocrites, and Bible thumpers. I wouldn't. I am so sorry to admit that there are people who claim to be Bible-believing Christians who totally misrepresent Christianity and what the Bible actually says. Some people see Christians as judgmental with holier-than-thou attitudes. There is nothing in the Bible, which is God's Word that supports or encourages Christ followers to carry out or display those attitudes and behaviors as listed above. For the non-believers and critics, is it fair to judge all Christians just based on a few people who claim to be Christians but they live their lives just the opposite? Is that judging the judging?

Now there are some Christians who know most of the Bible but may take verses out of context, not intentionally, but the message they are sharing is not what it really means. So it comes out twisted and misrepresents what the Bible actually says. Confusing? Yes, but it doesn't need to be.

#1. Hatred: Then there is the issue with hatred against particular individuals or group of people. God is our father, He made us. He does not hate us. He hates our behavior or any behavior that is against His will. Even though sin is sin, you can, however, find throughout the Bible strong emphasis put on some behaviors more than others.

> Don't you know that evil people won't have a share in the blessings of God's kingdom? Don't fool yourselves! No one who is immoral or worships idols or is unfaithful in marriage or is a pervert or behaves like a homosexual will share in God's kingdom. Neither will any thief or greedy person or drunkard or anyone who curses and cheats others. Some of you used to be like that. But now the name of our Lord Jesus Christ and the power of God's Spirit have washed you and made you holy and acceptable to God. (1 Corinthians 6:9–11 ERV)

God forgives all sins except for the rejection of Jesus Christ.

The Bible does not give Christians permission to hate others based on choices they make. Christians themselves are not perfect; however, we/they have been saved. That means we too have sinned (still do), but by accepting that Jesus Christ died on the cross to cover our sins, we are to repent (turn away from) and strive to walk daily as a witness for Jesus Christ. He came to save us not condemn us. So who are we to condemn? We are to love everyone, as humans in this sinful world that can very hard to do, but that does not mean we are to love the decisions that result in the bad behavior. Don't be confused. The Bible does not teach hatred toward people.

#2. Self-serving televangelist: We all know that there are people who portray themselves as godly Bible believers who use the media for their own selfish reasons and hidden agenda. Like those who build their own wealth by making you believe the Bible says it's okay. They tell you if you send money right now, you will be healed of your ailments. Jesus didn't charge money or ask people to pay him for healing them. In the history of television, there has also been many true godly Christians, Bible believers, evangelists, preachers, and teachers who really did and still do represent the Bible as God intended. The late Evangelist Billy Graham is the perfect example of how the Bible is to be represented. There are many more throughout history that should be credited as well, but there are too many to list in this book.

#3 Holier-than-thou: An attitude of being morally superior, judgmental, self-righteous, religious, better than you, artificial, and goody-goody.

Judgmental: Critical, finding-fault, condemning, disapproving, and negative. These are just a few words that describe being judgmental.

This is another group of *Christians* whose actions may confuse you. They view themselves as holier-than-thou. The ones who feel it's their duty to judge or try to control how people dress, wear their hair, or if they wear make-up. They tend to criticize people who even wear jewelry. Some will even disapprove of what you eat or drink, where you go, who you hang out with, if you go to church, and even what type of church you go to. How are we to be a witness to people who don't know Christ yet by condemning them?

We are not born Christians, and we as Christians are not perfect either. God did not give us the job to judge or condemn others for the decisions and choices they have made. We are to be a witness for Christ, guiding others to Christ. Once we have planted the seed, our Lord Jesus Christ is the only one to speak into the new believer's heart, mind, and soul. What others wear, eat, drink, and behaviors will change when the heart is changed if God sees fit for any changes to be made. Having long hair or short, wearing a long skirt or slacks, having a tattoo, or drinking a sip of wine is not going to keep you from being saved or going to heaven. Christians, when we see behavior that is not Christ-like, we need to look at ourselves and in our own hearts. We then can thank our Lord Jesus Christ for His forgiveness and pray for others to come to know Christ. Once you accept Jesus Christ, you do not *magically* change overnight. It is a lifetime of continuous growth. Everything you want and need to know about being a Christian is in the Bible. Don't let those behaviors confuse you, and please don't base your decision to come to Christ on just a few who may not fully understand what the Bible says. Here are a few verses concerning these things:

> Jesus said to him, "I am the way, and the truth, and the life. No one comes to the Father except through me. (John 14:6 NIV)

> Only Jesus has the power to save! His name is the only one in all the world that can save anyone. (Acts 4:12 CEV)

Keep in mind no matter how much someone else criticizes or judges, they do not have the power to save you or take you to heaven. And if you are the one doing the criticizing and judging, you need to have a talk with our Lord Jesus Christ and get into the word, the Word of God, the Holy Bible.

#4 Hypocrisy: A short word on how people view Christians as hypocrites, saying one thing but doing or living the opposite. It is also when people pretend to have moral or religious standards, but their behavior shows they do not. They seem to judge others for certain actions, but they do it themselves. They are not living out how the word of God instructs believers to live. That is really sad. If we as Jesus's followers are to be a witness to those who do not know Christ yet, then how can we truly be a witness if we say one thing but live our lives as if no one is watching. A few hypocrites do not represent all Christians. Listed are two verses on hypocrisy:

> You are hypocrites! Isaiah was right when he spoke for God about you: 'These people honor me with their words, but I am not really important to them. Their worship of me is worthless. The things they teach are only human rules. Matthew 15:7–9 (ERV)

> You hypocrite! First remove the beam from your own eye, and then you can see clearly to remove the speck from your brother's eye. (Matthew 7:5 NET)

> Do you suppose, O man—you who judge those who practice such things and yet do them yourself—that you will escape the judgment of God? (Romans 2:3 ESV)

#5 Bible thumpers: Now let me touch on the last Christian behavior that misrepresents the Bible that I have listed. These are just a few, and I am saddened to say there are probably many more. I don't know how many times I have heard people call Christians *bible thumpers*. These so-called Bible thumpers are labeled that because I truly believe with good intentions and from their heart, they want to share the Gospel. I know many well-meaning Christians who are so excited about how knowing Jesus Christ and how the Word of God can change lives they get so carried away and too aggressive. I would say when Christians are viewed as Bible thumpers, it takes on the impression of misrepresenting the Bible but not intentional. God wants us to share the gospel with patience, gentleness, and kindness.

The Bible says in 1 Peter 3:15 (ESV), "But in your hearts honor Christ the Lord as holy, always being prepared to make a defense to anyone who asks you for a reason for the hope that is in you; **yet do it with gentleness and respect** (in bold for emphasis).

I hope the explanations above will help you understand and encourage you to go forward in approaching the Bible with a different view. Maybe now you can come to the Holy Bible without the criticism based on the incorrect representation of the few.

CHAPTER 9

TAKEN OUT OF CONTEXT! WHAT DOES THAT MEAN?

Well, for example, and just for fun, because I enjoy baking, I am going to use the analogy of a recipe. I am sure if you took one ingredient out of a recipe (out of context) and baked it all by itself or used it the way you think it should be used, your recipe and final dish would totally be messed up and not make any sense. On top of that, it will probably taste yucky. Go ahead, bake one cup of flour. Stop. Just kidding, that doesn't make sense, don't do that. But now, do you see what I mean? Taking one word or sentence out of the *recipe*, it will taste yucky and not make any sense. You need all of the ingredients to make a good cake, one that make sense.

Taken out of context is when *words, verses, terms, quotes, names, or titles taken out of context, abused, misused, and confused.*

I have provided two definitions for the meaning of *taking out of context* from our most reliable sources.

1. Merriam-Webster: If the words that someone has said are taken or quoted "out of context," they are repeated without explaining the situation in which they were said so that their meaning is changed.
2. Longman Dictionary of Contemporary English: To take or quote something *out of context*, to repeat part of what

someone has said or written without describing the situation in which it was said so that it means something quite different.

This has become my pet peeve. However, I know I have been guilty of this myself. But after much studying, reading, learning, and experiencing it personally, I found out how important it is not to practice this and why taking words out of context can cause confusion. Set aside the Bible for a minute. Now think about the last book, any book, magazine, a bill, a recipe, or just about anything you have read or heard. Now apply the idea of taking what you read or what you heard out of context. Or maybe you too have had an experience when you had told someone something that was important to you, but what you had told them got twisted or *taken out of context* and was retold in a manner that did not reflect what you said at all or only part of what you said was repeated. Annoying!

What you said was taken out of context. What you meant to say ended up being told by the other person what they wanted it to mean by using only a part of what you said. As you see, it can make all the difference. Especially when reading the Bible. It may or may not be intentional, but people tend to take Bible verses out of context to abuse or misuse to fit what they want it to say or mean. This is what we do to God's Word, the Bible. Let me remind you again, you *cannot* change the meaning of what the author meant. Here are four examples of verses that are continually taken out of context provided from different Bible versions.

First example:

New Testament Luke 4:7 (KJV) reads, "If thou therefore wilt worship me, all shall be thine."

New Testament Luke 4:7 (ESV) reads, "If you, then, will worship me, it will all be yours."

What do you think this verse means?

Write down what you understand, or how did you *interpret* that verse?

Do you see how this verse can mean something else when taken out of context?

Like a lot of people, reading this out of context or not reading the verses before and after, you may think our Lord Jesus Christ was telling us, the reader, that if we worship Him, He will gives us everything we want. *Not!* Read on.

New Testament Luke 4:8 (KJV) reads, "And Jesus answered and said unto him, 'Get thee behind me, Satan: for it is written, Thou shalt worship the Lord thy God, and him only shalt thou serve.'"

New Testament Luke 4:8 (ESV) reads, "And Jesus answered him, It is written, 'You shall worship the Lord your God, and him only shall you serve.'"

As you see, Satan was trying to tempt Jesus. It had nothing to do with Jesus telling us if we worship Him He will give us everything.

Second example:

New Testament Philippians 4:13 (NLT) reads, "For I can do everything through Christ, who gives me strength."

New Testament Philippians 4:13 (KJV) reads, "I can do all things through Christ which strengthens me."

What do you think this verse means?

Take a few moments, and write down how you *interpreted* this verse.

No, this does not mean you can run outside and lift your car up over your head. *No*, this does not mean you can go pass your exam without any effort on your part. *No*, this does not mean we can be superhuman just because we have Christ in our life. Yes, God can and will give us strength beyond our understanding in his timing.

Context: The Apostle Paul was speaking to the Philippians about how he was enduring hardships as a result of living out his faith. Read New Testament Philippians 4:10 through 4:15.

> I rejoiced in the Lord greatly that now at length you have revived your concern for me. You were indeed concerned for me, but you had no opportunity. Not that I am speaking of being in need, for I have learned in whatever situation I am to be content. I know how to be brought low, and I know how to abound. In any and every circumstance, I have learned the secret of facing plenty and hunger, abundance and need. I can do all things through him who strengthens me.
>
> Yet it was kind of you to share my trouble. And you Philippians yourselves know that in the beginning of the gospel, when I left Macedonia, no church entered into partnership with me in giving and receiving, except you only. (New Testament Philippians 4:10–15 ESV)

We can do a lot, go through many trials, experience grief, and come to the other end with the strength that God alone can offer us. We will endure hardship and challenges when living out our faith for Christ.

I recommend reading the book of Philippians, all of chapter 4 for the full meaning to lessen the confusion about that particular verse.

Third example:

"God will never give you more than you can handle." This quote is not even in the Bible. This quote is not necessarily taken out of context. It is just misquoted to suit our needs.

New Testament 1 Corinthians 10:13 (NLT) reads, "The temptations in your life are no different from what others experience. And God is faithful. He will not allow the temptation to be more than you can stand. When you are tempted, he will show you a way out so that you can endure."

New Testament 1 Corinthians 10:13 (KJV) reads, "There hath no temptation taken you but such as is common to man: but God is faithful, who will not suffer you to be tempted above that ye are able; but will with the temptation also make a way to escape, that ye may be able to bear it."

Fourth example:

This one has been taken out of context and probably abused and misused the most by believers and non-believers and Christians and non-Christians. This verse can be confusing when you don't fully understand the context in which it was written and the message the writer was telling us.

New Testament Ephesians 5:22 (KJV) reads, "Wives, submit yourselves unto your own husbands…"

New Testament Ephesians 5:22 (ESV) reads, "Wives, submit to your own husbands…"

New Testament Ephesians 5:22 (CEV) reads, "A wife should put her husband first…"

What do you think this verse is saying?

Read the complete verse.

New Testament Ephesians 5:22 (KJV) reads, "Wives submit to yourselves unto your own husbands, as to the Lord."

New Testament Ephesians 5:22 (ESV) reads, "Wives submit to you own husbands, as to the Lord."

New Testament Ephesians 5:22 (CEV) reads, "A wife should put her husband first, as she does the Lord."

Now after you have read the complete verse, do you feel the meaning was changed?

The meaning is not complete without the following verses:

> For the husband is the head of the wife, even as Christ is the head of the church: and he is the Savior of the body. Therefore as the church is subject unto Christ, so let the wives be to their own husbands in everything. Husbands, love your wives, even as Christ also loved the church, and gave himself for it. (Ephesians 5:23–25 KJV)

> For the husband is the head of the wife as Christ is the head of the church, his body, and himself its Savior. Now as the church submits to Christ, so also wives should submit in everything to their husbands. Husbands, love your wives, as Christ loved the church and gave himself up for her. (Ephesians 5:23–25 ESV)

A husband is the head of his wife, as Christ is the head and the Savior of the church, which is his own body. Wives should always put their husbands first, as the church puts Christ first. A husband should love his wife as much as Christ loved the church and gave his life for it. (Ephesians 5:23–25 CEV)

However, let each one of you love his wife as himself, and let the wife see that she respects her husband. (Ephesians 5:33 CEV)

A brief summary from the verses you just read:

You will not find anywhere in these verses does God give permission for a husband or wife to be in charge, mistreat, degrade, disrespect, or be unloving. Your spouse, wife (female) or husband (male), is not your slave. God is instructing the husband to love his wife like Jesus loves us, His church. Wives respect your husband the way Jesus respects His church, His followers. I hope this explanation cleared up the confusion about the verses that has been and still is taken out of context. Side note: There are at least one hundred verses in the Bible about marriage between one man and one woman. The husband is a man, and the wife is woman. God's design. No confusion.

You can choose to agree or disagree, but you still can't change the meaning of what the author meant. God is the author (https://www.openbible.info/topics/marriage_between_one_man_and_one_woman).

To get the full understanding of the verses you just read, go back, and read Ephesians chapter 5 verses 1 through 33.

Okay, so no more cheating. I gave you the verses in the examples above to give you an idea of how to do these exercises. Look up and read the verse first, and then read the full chapter or the related verses listed below.

Read the verse, and write down what you think the verse means. After you have written down what you think it means, read the chapter or related verses, and then re-write what the author meant to say before the verse was taken out of context.

New Testament Matthew 7:1 (NLT) reads, "Do not judge others, and you will not be judged."
What do you think this means?

_____

Now read Matthew 7:1–5 any version. Write the meaning of what the author meant.

_____

Old Testament Jeremiah 29:11 (NIV) reads, "For I know the plans I have for you," declares the Lord, "plans to prosper you and not to harm you, plans to give you hope and a future."

Write down how you feel about this verse or what you think it means.

_____

Read Jeremiah 29:1–14 any version. You will read a brief history behind this statement where the Lord is speaking to the people of Israel who been taken to Babylon as captives. But as you continue to read on through verse 14, you will find in verse 12 that God made a promise to the ones who seek Him.
Now read chapter 29 verses 1–14. Write down in a few sentences what you understand now from verse 11 and what it means after it has been put back into the context in which it was meant.

_____

_____

Can you see how it can change the meaning of what the author actually meant when taken out of context?

Now, I hope you understand why the Bible may seem confusing. Well, it is not always the Bible that is confusing, it is the way we read it. Don't just read a verse or part of the chapter if you want to know the full meaning. However, there are verses in the Bible that can be read and clearly understood within the one or two verses. And there will be some verses that can and will be difficult to understand. Some are very clear as what the author meant without reading the full chapter. Flat out, some verses mean what it says and says what it was meant to say. It would be difficult to take them out of context to mean anything else. You have probably seen examples such as *Bible Verse of the Day* (https://biblestudytools.com, https://bible.com) and *Today's Devotional* (https://odb.org Our Daily Bread online), as pop-ups or listed in publications. Here are a few verses out of many that you can read as standalone and get the full meaning.

> For God so loved the world that he gave his one and only Son, that whoever believes in him shall not perish but have eternal life. (John 3:16 NIV)

> In the beginning God created the heavens and the earth. (Genesis 1:1 NLT)

> All scripture is given by inspiration of God, and is profitable for doctrine, for reproof, for correction, for instruction in righteousness. (2 Timothy 3:16 KJV)

Stop here for a minute. I know this is a lot to take in, take a break, breath. Try to remember a conversation you have had or statement you have made and the end result was nothing close to what you meant to say. That probably hurt your feelings sometimes too.

Does anyone have the authority to change the meaning of what you meant to say?

When you feel you are sharing God's Word with good intentions, but the information is taken out of context, the full meaning can ultimately be misapplied and cause your intended witness to go astray or be misunderstood by a non-believer or new believer resulting in rejection or disbelieve. As Christians, we are called to share God's Word and to spread the gospel, so don't be afraid when the opportunity is presented. Just ask the Holy Spirit to help guide you in relaying the message and the meaning of what the author meant not what we think it means.

Now you see why it is very important to know the verses' full meaning. It will help you understand better so that you will no longer be confused.

Of course, I do not guarantee you will understand everything you read. It will take some time and effort on your part if you really want to enjoy discovering the Bible with a new perspective and learn that you can trust the Bible to be true.

CHAPTER 10

WHY DO I NEED TO KNOW "WHO BEGAT WHO?"

I t's genealogy! Well, what is genealogy?

1. A record or account of the ancestry of a person, family, group, etc.
2. The study of family ancestries and histories (https://www.dictionary.com/browse/genealogy).

There are many companies these days that sell a variety of software programs that can help you build a family tree or find an ancestor. You may be curious about your heritage, where your family originated, or who was married to whom or *who begat who*. Am I related to someone famous? Maybe you are a descendent of a king or queen. Or maybe a scientist, an artist, or a farmer. When you do find something out about them, it can be exciting. Do you have a special trait and finally discovered who you inherited that trait from? You may even find out it is someone you don't really want to be related to. Yikes! You don't have to tell anyone. Laugh, it's okay. You can't change it.

It was of the highest importance to the people of ancient Israel to know who their ancestors were. Way before the internet, search engines, and ancestry software, people took great pain in keeping detailed records that preserve the family tree.

Several versions of the Bible use the term *begat*. Allow me to briefly explain what *begat* means according to scripture. You can find the word *bare* in the book of Genesis. When Leah, in Genesis 46:15, bare sons and daughters, the Hebrew word *yalad* is translated as begat, so Leah begat children. Today we would say that Leah gave birth to children. Just as all birth mothers begat their children. The Bible Dictionary states, "To bear; bring forth." The Bible will also use the term mostly when talking about the male descendants, not that the men physically gave birth, we know that.

> The book of the generation of Jesus Christ, the son of David, the son of Abraham. Abraham begat Isaac; and Isaac begat Jacob; ...And Jesse begat David the king; (generations later) And Jacob begat Joseph the husband of Mary, of whom was born Jesus, who is called Christ. (Matthew 1:1–17 KJV)

There are several reasons why we should be familiar with why there is a long list of generations listed in the Bible. You don't need to know or memorize each and every person, child, grandchild, great-grandchild, father, grandfather, great-grandfather, mother, grandmother, and great-grandmother in the Bible. It's hard enough to memorize or even be a little familiar with our own list of generations and ancestors. Two books of the Bible that contain records of descendants in the Old Testament are Genesis and Numbers. There are a few more. In these two books, you will find the family tree starting with Adam and Eve, the family of Moses, and Noah and his family after the flood. If this is something that really sparks your interest, you could search back far enough to find out which son of Noah you descended from.

Read Genesis 7:13. Can you list the names of Noah's three sons:

1._____ 2. _____ 3. _____

Many books of the OT have lists of worthy ancestors that were used to determine if you were in line to become a priest or a king. Their heredity also determined military duty. You can find much of that information in the books of Exodus, Numbers, 1 Chronicles, and Ezra. There are several more books that have a short list of ancestry but just as important. The Gospels of Matthew and Luke in the NT describe the lineage of Jesus.

Can you think of any reason you might want to know who your ancestors are? You can use the space below to write those reasons down.

_____

_____

_____

When you count back from how many years your father lived, then his father lived, then his father lived, and so on, you can get an idea of a generation timeline. How many years did you count backward?

One very big important factor with the generations listed, who begat who, and how long they lived, we have a timeline that traces back to the beginning of mankind, Adam and Eve. Bible scholars, believers, non-believers, and scientist of different beliefs have used the dates of birth, length of life, and deaths to build a timeline to date back to Adam. How many years from the beginning to now? This is how we get the approximate years dating back to Adam and Eve. Not billions of years. Many scholars, historians, archeologist, theologians, geologist, scientist, and people who study chronology agree God created Adam and Eve around four thousand years before the birth of Christ which is about six thousand years ago. See Answers in Genesis.org/bible-timeline/. I highly suggest visiting the Creation Museum in Petersburg, Kentucky (www.creationmuseum.org).

The beginning of the generations can be found in Genesis 5:1 (ESV), "This is the book of generations of Adam. When God created man, he made him in the likeness of God." You will find in the book of Genesis the ancestors from Adam to Noah and then Noah to Abram (God later changed his name to Abraham).

The book of Numbers is important because this is where Moses and the people of Israel escaped Egypt, also known as the Exodus. The Lord ordered Moses to take a head count so that Moses would know the number of people in each of the twelve tribes and assign their duty.

For simplicity sake and not to cause confusion, the information provided for this topic is the short and simple version. You could spend hours and hours on this subject of *who begat who*.

These are just several reasons why it is important to know why the books of the Bible contain genealogies or so-called who begat who. The most important of all is the line of Jesus. The Bible records the legal ancestry of Jesus through Joseph as well as the blood line of Jesus through Mary, His birth mother.

The ancestry of Jesus shows He is in the legal line from Joseph which is explained in the book of Matthew starting in chapter 1 verse 1–17. Joseph is a descendant of David, and David is a descendant of Abraham. Of course the family tree goes further back, all the way to God, our creator.

Joseph was Jesus's step-father because Jesus was born of the Virgin Mary, His birth mother, but His father was God himself. Then there is the ancestry of Jesus from the lineage of His birth mother Mary, the virgin.

There are two different genealogy branches for Jesus just like there are for you and me. There is one from the father and one from the mother.

For the list of descendants from Adam and Eve to the sons of Noah, read Genesis 5:1–32. Genesis is the first book of the Bible, chapter 5, verses 1 through 32. Then you can read about the generations from Noah's sons starting in Genesis 10:1 through Genesis 46:27 to include the descendants and family of Joseph the legal father of Jesus.

The lineage of Jesus going back to Abraham through King David is shown in the family tree illustration.

Read Genesis 21:3. Can you list the name of Abraham and Sarah's son?

1._____

Read Genesis 25:21. Can you list the names of the two grandsons of Abraham and Sarah?

1._____ 2. _____

JESUS' FAMILY TREE

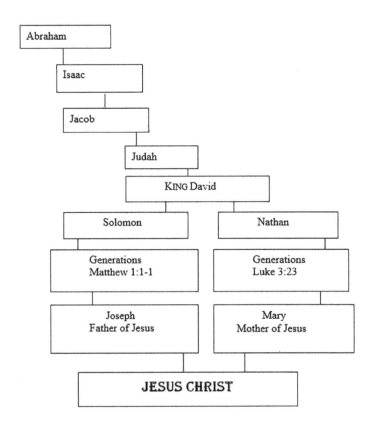

There are multiple accounts recorded about the birth of Jesus in the Bible and outside of the Bible as well. In the New Testament, the book of Matthew 1:18—22 (ESV) reads, "Now the birth of Jesus Christ took place in this way. When his mother Mary had been betrothed to Joseph, before they came together she was found to be with child from the Holy Spirit. And her husband Joseph, being a just man and unwilling to put her to shame, resolved to divorce her quietly. But as he considered these things, behold, an angel of the Lord appeared to him in a dream, saying, 'Joseph, son of David, do not fear to take Mary as your wife, for that which is conceived in her is from the Holy Spirit. She will bear a son, and you shall call his name Jesus, for he will save his people from their sins.' All this took place to fulfill what the Lord had spoken by the prophet..."

Old Testament prophecy in Isaiah 7:14 (NIV) reads, "Therefore the Lord himself will give you a sign: The virgin shall conceive and give birth to a son, and will call him Immanuel."

A final note about why the Bible has the genealogies and the long list of ancestries, it is God's way of showing us that He used people from all walks of life, ages, time periods, and experiences to tell his story. *And* here is a bonus, with the *who begat who*, we can trace back to Adam and Eve which reveals the approximate age of the earth to be six thousand years, not billions. Start with the book of Genesis. Adam and Eve are the parents of *who begat who*. As God is the author of the Bible, He is the creator of all.

I hope this lesson was fun and provided an answer to the question *why do I need to know who begat who?*

It may not have answered all of your questions due to the fact that the Bible has a very long history and thousands of years of generations. The topic deserves more time and space than we can cover in this book.

CHAPTER 11

WHAT DOES THE OLD TESTAMENT HAVE TO DO WITH THE NEW TESTAMENT? HOW DO THEY CONNECT?

That is a good question. You are not alone in asking this. You may be a little confused or just curious. How does the Old Testament and the New Testament connect?

We can't have a complete Bible without the New Testament connecting to the Old Testament. It would not be a complete book. The Old Testament books *do* connect with the New Testament books. There are many ways.

Write down in your own words what you feel about how the Old Testament connects to the New Testament.

I have heard people make comments about how the Old Testament is just a bunch of scary stories, myths, fairy tales, and brutality. Some of that is true but only the scary stories and brutality. The Bible is a book of reality, both the Old Testament and the New Testament. Life is full of scary stuff and brutality. The Bible is also full of the reality of grace, love, patience, kindness, forgiveness, and sacrifice.

You may already know the majority of the Bible is made up of the Old Testament with thirty-nine books. The New Testament has twenty-seven books. There is a good reason for that. The Old Testament history is longer and has much more to say to prepare you for the New Testament. Don't forget, God is the ultimate author of the Bible, both the Old Testament and the New Testament. God is love. God does not lie. God is not a God of confusion. God is perfect.

> For God is not a God of confusion but of
> peace. (1 Corinthians 14:33 ESV)

The overall story of the Old Testament is simple, but each book can be complicated. So beginning with the book of Genesis through to the last book of the Old Testament book of Micah, we will look at it as an overview.

The Old Testament starts with the beginning of creation. All creation. As you proceed, you will read about the unfolding of the promise God made to the people of Israel. The Old Testament is the history of real people, their daily lives, ups and downs, choices they made for good and evil, spiritual warfare, and choosing to obey or disobey God. They had to make decisions that affected them just like we do. They had families to take care of. They had to figure out how to get food, what to wear, where to live, who was assigned certain chores or jobs, and which male family member had to go off to war. They had to deal with extreme weather, natural disasters, and all the physical challenges we have today.

The people in the Old Testament also dealt with temptation, sexual immorality, alcohol abuse, prejudices, poverty, and many other human situations known to us. And just because bad choices were made by the people in the Bible, does not mean God approved or gave his blessings on those decisions. You will also find that God blessed those who obeyed Him, and they were thankful for their many blessings. God is the creator and Father of all humans, and as a father, He does reprimand and discipline. We all have to pay the consequences for our actions, and sometimes we even have to suffer for the decisions others make. Just like good earthly parents, once a child knows right from wrong and still makes a decision to do the wrong thing, most likely the child will be disciplined. God did not create us to be robots. He gave us a free will with the ability to make our own decisions as human beings. Just like those who lived from the time of Adam and Eve and up to today.

The Old Testament is the history of events and stories of the people preparing for the coming of the Messiah, the Savior. It tells of how God is revealing His love and His saving grace through the lives of the people who continued to disobey His commands. There are stories of many people who did listen to God and who loved and obeyed His commands, and for that, they received many blessings.

In the Old Testament, you will see that clean animals were sacrificed over and over for sin and rebellion. In the New Testament, Jesus was the final sacrifice. So there was no longer the need to sacrifice animals for sin. He gave his life for the sin of rebellious mankind. The New Testament is the story about Jesus, His birth, life, death, and resurrection. We no longer have to sacrifice animals for our wrongdoing. Jesus was the Messiah, the Savior that the Old Testament talked about from Genesis to the last book of Malachi. His story is the beginning of the New Testament and the beginning of Christianity. The Old Testament promise is full-filled by the arrival of Jesus Christ.

During Jesus's earthly ministry, He often referred to and used the scriptures of the Old Testament with authority. Apostles, disciples, and followers of Jesus Christ also referred to the scriptures of the Old Testament when speaking to folks in their day and carried those over in their books or letters. There are many passages in the New Testament that speak of the Old Testament and what God was revealing to us.

The table below will also display how the Old and New Testament connect.

Here are a few verses in the left column from the Old Testament that were written hundreds of years before and by various people chosen by God. The writers in the New Testament are emphasizing what God had told us in the Old Testament, while other OT writers and prophets are declaring what God had revealed to them of what will transpire in the NT.

Old Testament	New Testament

Genesis 1:27 NKJV
    So God created man in His own image; in the image of God He created him; male and female He created them.
	Mark 10:6 NKJV
	    But from the beginning of the creation, God 'made them male and female.'

Deuteronomy 32:35 CEV
    Soon our enemies will get what they deserve—suddenly they will slip, and total disaster will quickly follow.
	Romans 12:19 CEV
	    Dear friends, don't try to get even. Let God take revenge. In the Scriptures the Lord says, "I am the one to take revenge and pay them back."

Isaiah 7:14 ASV
    Therefore the Lord himself will give you a sign. Behold, the virgin shall conceive and bear a son, and shall call his name Immanuel.
	Luke 2:7 and 11 ASV
	    And she brought forth her firstborn son; for there is born to you this day in the city of David a Saviour, who is Christ the Lord.

Leviticus 23:19 KJV
    Then ye shall sacrifice one kid of the goats for a sin offering, and two lambs of the first year for a sacrifice of peace offerings.
	Hebrews 10:10 NLT
	    For God's will was for us to be made holy by the sacrifice of the body of Jesus Christ, once for all time.

Exodus 31:18 NIV
    When the Lord finished speaking to Moses on Mount Sinai, he gave him the two tablets of the covenant law, the tablets of stone inscribed by the finger of God.
	Matthew 5:17 ESV
	    "Do not think that I have come to abolish the Law or the Prophets; I have not come to abolish then but the fulfill them."

Deuteronomy 29:9 ESV
    Therefore keep the words of this covenant and do them, that you may prosper in all that you do.
    (Physical blessings)
	Ephesians 1:3 NASB
	    Blessed be the God and the Father of our Lord Jesus Christ, who has blessed us with every spiritual blessing in the heavenly places in Christ.
	    (Spiritual blessings)

The New Testament has not totally been full-filled and will not until the return of Jesus Christ and when the book of Revelation has come to completion. The New Testament starts with the book of Matthew and ends with the book of Revelation. To sum up the book of Revelation, it is the past, present, and future of mankind and the world.

My suggestion is to wait until you get comfortable reading the Bible before you try to read the book of Revelation. I cannot stress this more, you do need the Holy Spirit to help guide you when you are reading the Bible for the fullness that God, the author, meant it to be.

Here is an analogy of how you can connect the new to the old. It is something simple that you may be able to relate to. We are looking to buy a house, and let's say that the house was built a long time ago. You want to make sure the house has a really good solid foundation.

That solid foundation is the Old Testament scriptures. God is the builder of the Old Testament foundation. Stories and lives of many people over many years have come and gone. This old house is worn out and waiting to be saved, remodeled, and renewed.

Now we have the New Testament scriptures. God is the builder of the New Testament that completes this house through Jesus Christ. To be saved, remodeled, and renewed, we need to put on a new roof, new walls, and then re-do the inside. We did not do away with the *foundation*. We built on the foundation.

God is the foundation. Jesus is the roof, and the Holy Spirit is the walls. We need to look on the inside of our *house* at ourselves and accept the Old Testament with the New Testament. You need a strong foundation to put the walls and roof on. You cannot have one part without the other. We need a strong foundation with a roof and walls, just like we need God, our Father; His Son, Jesus Christ; and the Holy Spirit. We need the Old Testament scriptures to go with our New Testament scriptures like we need the New Testament scriptures to complete the Old Testament scriptures.

You may notice a little pattern here. I love telling stories with analogies, being able to tell a story with something that you can relate to. Jesus used parables as a way of telling a story, almost like an analogy, except a parable is used for a spiritual or moral lesson.

So here is one more example if you enjoy the art of baking.

I have several family members who love carrot cake, so I am going to use it for the recipe.

First half of the recipe: flour, baking soda, baking powder, salt, cinnamon, eggs, oil, and sugar.

Second half of the recipe: crushed pineapple, shredded carrots, and walnut pieces.

Of course the cream cheese icing to top it off.

Just like the Old Testament is the first half. New Testament is the second half, and then Revelation is to top it off.

So now you may have some insight of how the Old Testament relates to the New Testament. However, this is not a complete picture of how they connect, but I want to keep it simple. This analogy is just to give you a brief idea of how the two come together. They do connect to create the full book of the Bible. You really do need more time and deserve more attention than this book can cover.

CHAPTER 12

A JOURNEY THROUGH THE BIBLE IS LIKE GOING ON A WORLD CRUISE!

I am so excited. But you may be thinking you don't want to cruise or you do not like being on the water. Well, that's okay, just sail with me here, and you will understand what I mean. If you do like the idea of a world cruise, then grab your passport/Bible, and let's start our journey. Whether this is your first time or have taken many trips from Genesis to Revelation, this experience will give you a new and exciting way of looking at the bible. You don't need to be confused to go on a cruise or read through your bible. Also keep in mind, unless you personally set a goal or time limit to read through the Bible, we are in no hurry. Relax and enjoy.

The Bible consist of sixty-six *books*, so for the purpose of the world cruise, we can look at them as ports, cities, villages, towns, islands, and even fjords. The books of the Bible are also diverse in its journey, but overall it is one big journey just like a world cruise from beginning to end. While you are cruising, you may want to jot down notes or keep a journal of your trip to refer back to when your journey ends. This will be a reminder of your favorite book or village that you want to return to first.

This world cruise is a *fun-made-up* cruise just to give you an idea of the different places you can go to in one journey from beginning to end. When you take a world cruise, you make brief stops or visits at each port, island, city, town, or village to get a taste of what it's like. Then after you finish and return home, you can choose from a variety of those stops to return to for a much longer visit to really get to know the culture, language, food, celebrations, history, and so on. It is almost the same as reading the bible from Genesis to Revelation. You will read through with a brief stay in each book of the Bible.

After you have read through it, then go back to any one of the books to study deeper, spend some quality time, and get to know the history, culture, time period, geography, foods, the people, characters, and what God is revealing to us through that particular book of the bible. But like a world cruise, there will be waves of ups and downs that you may experience while reading particular books, chapters, or verses along the journey. Just hold on, the big waves don't last long. The book of Revelation is for the more experienced traveler, so save that part of the journey for the last stop.

As you would have a captain of a ship, we have God as the captain of the Bible.

1. Hawaiian Islands 2. Alaska 3. Los Angeles 4. Mexico 5. Peru 6. Argentina 7. Brazil 8. Caribbean 9. New York 10. Canada 11. Greenland 12. Netherlands 12. Norway 13. Ireland/the United Kingdom 14. Spain 15. Morocco 16. South Africa 17. Madagascar 18. To Egypt 19. India 20. Sri Lanka 21. Indonesia 22. Australia 23. New Zealand 24. Great Barrier Reef 25. Papua New Guinea 26. The Philippines 27. Japan 28. Russia

This fun world cruise has taken you to continents, countries, states, cities, villages, towns, and islands. When visiting all of these places, you would experience a very wide range of foods, culture, languages, habitats, religions, geography, history, time zones, and diversity of every kind. You probably found that you enjoyed some of these places so much that you would like to go back and make your visit longer so that you have time to learn more about those destinations.

That is like taking a journey through the Bible. You begin your journey in Genesis, making short stops along the way in the books of the Bible. Within the different books of the Bible, you will find, if you haven't already, that the Bible is full of history, geography, multiple locations, culture, time periods, battles, people groups, landscape, weather, epic natural phenomenon, miracles, mysteries unfolding, religion, and so much more. After breezing through from Genesis to Revelation on your journey, go back and start reading a particular book of interest, and take your time. Stay in that *port* for a while so that you can learn and enjoy.

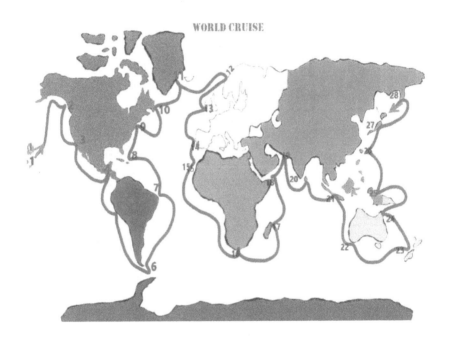

WORLD CRUISE

CHAPTER 13

OLD TESTAMENT BIBLE JOURNEY MAP WITH KEY FOLLOW THE BOOKS OF THE BIBLE ON THE MAP

The stops are numbered in order as you come to the books in the Bible. Each stop may have more than one book to visit, so you may be there a short time, or you may be there longer.

Each location is the general area where the book was written or event happened. The book of Job and Obadiah does not provide evidence of the exact location but based on information that most closely identifies with that area during that period of time. When you get to the book of Psalms, there is not just one location because several people from numerous places and time periods contributed to this book. However, since King David and King Solomon wrote most of the Psalms, we will put the location as Israel.

Locations used are based on scripture writings and history as recorded in the Bible. Some locations are not exact. Below is a description of how to go on this journey through the Old Testament locations on the map.

Departure point for this journey is A—beginning in the Old Testament with the thirty-nine books. The books are numbered in order as you read through the Bible. For the letter A, the first five books of the Bible were written by Moses while he was in the

Wilderness. Then follow the arrow to letter B. From the book of Joshua all the way to the book of Nehemiah, they were either written or the event happened in the areas of Israel/Canaan/Judah. Next, you would follow the arrow to C which is Persia and so on. When you continue to follow the arrows through to the letter J, you will end at the last book of Old Testament which is Malachi.

A. The wilderness/Egypt
1. Genesis
2. Exodus
3. Leviticus
4. Numbers
5. Deuteronomy

B. Israel/Canaan/Judah
6. Joshua
7. Judges
8. Ruth
9 & 10. 1 and 2 Samuel
11 & 12. 1 and 2 Kings
13 & 14. 1 and 2 Chronicles
15. Ezra
16. Nehemiah

C. Persia
17. Esther

D. Land of Uz
18. Job

E. Israel/Canaan/Judah
19. Psalms
20. Proverbs
21. Ecclesiastes
22. Song of Songs/Song Solomon

23. Isaiah
24. Jeremiah

F. Babylon
25. Lamentations
26. Ezekiel
27. Daniel

G. Israel/Canaan/Judah
28. Hosea
29. Joel
30. Amos

H. Edom
31. Obadiah

I. Nineveh
32. Jonah

J. Israel/Canaan/Judah
33. Micah
34. Nahum
35. Habakkuk
36. Zephaniah
37. Haggai
38. Zechariah
39. Malachi

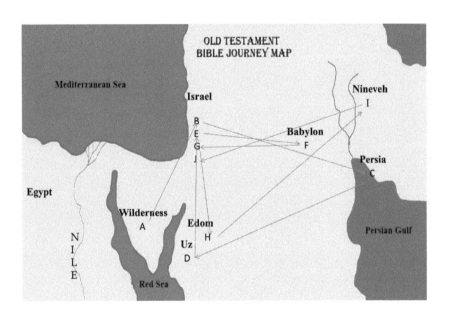

CHAPTER 14

NEW TESTAMENT BIBLE JOURNEY MAP WITH KEY FOLLOW THE BOOKS OF THE BIBLE ON THE MAP

The books are numbered in order as you come to them in the New Testament. This map does not have the arrows because there are so many that go back and forth. It would be confusing. The location for the book of Hebrews is not stated in the Bible, but it is clear it was written to the Hebrew people. So we will place it in Israel for the purpose of the map. The location for the book of Jude is also not known, but scholars identify him as being related to Jesus. So we will place this book in Israel as well. This Bible map takes you on a journey through the twenty-seven books of the New Testament. You will start at the letter A with the book of Matthew, and then find the letter B for the book of Mark. The next book takes you back to the letter A for the next three books. Continue following the list which will take you to each location on the map until your journey ends at the letter F, which is the book of Revelation. The books are numbered 1–27. Each location on the map is where the books were written based on the information derived from the Bible or archeological finds.

A. Israel
  1. Matthew
  3. Luke
  4. John
  5. Acts 1–12 (1)
  19. Hebrews
  20. James
  26. Jude

B. Rome
  2. Mark
  5. Acts 21–28 (4)
  9. Galatians
  10. Ephesians
  11. Philippians
  12. Colossians
  15. 1 Timothy
  16. 2 Timothy
  17. Titus
  18. Philemon
  21. 1 Peter
  22. 2 Peter

C. Antioch
  5. Acts 13–18 (2)

D. Greece
  6. Romans
  13. 1 Thessalonians
  14. 2 Thessalonians
  8. 2 Corinthians

E. Ephesus
  5. Acts 19–21 (3)
  7. 1 Corinthians
  23. 1 John

24. 2 John
25. 3 John

F. Island of Patmos
27. Revelation

SHARON ROSE

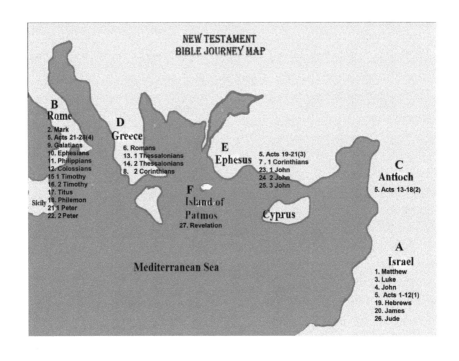

96

NOW PLAN HOW YOU WANT TO JOURNEY THROUGH THE BIBLE

There are many different ways to read through the Bible. Starting at Genesis and going through to the book Revelation is just one option. I chose this reading plan for fun and to use as a comparison on a map. Many Bibles have ideas and suggested ways to read through it by following a plan. You can decide which plan best fits you. Knowing where the people were when they were writing the Scriptures or where the events were taking place may help you understand the Bible a little more than you did before.

And now here is another trip for you, a guilt trip. Just kidding. We probably all have made this excuse of why we don't read the bible, "Oh I don't have time." I was guilty of this as well. *But* looking back, how much time did I spend watching television, chatting, cooking, cleaning, shopping, and so on? How many times can you remember complaining about sitting in the doctor's office waiting and waiting? Wasted time? Lately, for most of us, its social media; texting; online shopping; reading magazines, books, and other written material; and playing games on our phones, tablets, and variety of electronics. We can, if we want, cut out a few minutes or more a day to read God's Word, the Bible.

And if you don't enjoy reading or your eyes just get too tired, no problem. There are numerous apps that you can download to your electronic device that is an audio version of the Bible. So now you can listen to the Bible as well. Make sure you select the version you can relate to the most from the lesson about versions earlier in this book. Let me suggest that you listen to a few before purchasing. I had one where the narrator sound like he just came right out of some dramatic movie. Some people may enjoy that and some may not.

WRAPPING IT UP

Now that you have read through this book and hopefully participated in the activities, are you ready to start reading and enjoying your own Bible? You may want to find a favorite quiet spot in the house, backyard, patio, a coffee shop, or peaceful hiding place to read. You can use the same place, same time, or just wherever and whenever you can.

I want to challenge you right now to start your journey. If you already have a Bible, find the plan that fits your life style. If you don't have a Bible yet, then go back to the chapter called *Which Version of the Bible Should I Read?* and compare the different versions. Then you can also find the reading plan that fits in with your everyday life.

As we are wrapping this up, I want to share this story about a gift.

At Christmas time, there is a present under the tree. Someone who loves you very much offers you the gift. Now you decide to accept the gift or not. God gave His only son, Jesus Christ, as a gift to us, but He doesn't make us take it, we have to want it. Inside the wrapping is the gift of forgiveness. Accepting that gift from God is the only way to heaven. Just like at Christmas time, we know about gifts. We may even know what is in the wrapped gift, but knowing is not the same as accepting and receiving. We need to be thankful for this wonderful gift of Jesus Christ from the Father, Lord our God. I pray that everyone who has not accepted this gift from our Lord, the gift of our Savior Jesus Christ, do so now.

This book would not be complete without touching on how the topic of how heaven can be confusing. There are many, but here are a few verses from the Bible about heaven. Remember, I did not write the Bible. God is the author of the Bible. This is what the

Bible says about the gift of eternal life and the Kingdom of God as referring to heaven.

> For God so loved the world, that He gave his only begotten Son, that whoever believeth in him should not perish but have everlasting life. For God did not send his Son into the world to condemn the world; but that the world through him might be saved. (John 3:16–17 KJV)

> For by grace have ye been saved through faith; and that not of yourselves, *it is* the gift of God; not of works, that no man should glory. (Ephesians 2:8–9 ASV)

> Sin pays off with death. But God's gift is eternal life given by Jesus Christ our Lord. (Romans 6:23 CEV)

> Jesus answered him, "Truly, truly, I say to you, unless one is born again he cannot see the kingdom of God." (John 3:3 ESV)

For more detailed truths about heaven, read the book *Heaven* by Randy Alcorn.

Thank you for taking the time out of your busy life to read this book. My prayer is that you will now be inspired to open the pages and not be as confused about the Bible as you once were.

Give thanks to the one and only author, our Lord God Almighty.

DEFINITIONS AND DESCRIPTIONS

AD: From the Latin phrase Anno Domini which means The Year of our Lord. AD is placed before the number of the year.

"AD 1" See Fun Facts

Amen: Used after prayers to show agreement of what has been said and have faith that it will happen.

Angel: Created by God to serve as God's messenger. Angels are heavenly, spiritual, powerful protectors, and holy beings. Angels are God's servants and not to be worshiped. Angels are present throughout the Old Testament and the New Testament. Angels are mentioned in the Bible approximately three hundred times.

Anoint: Miriam-Webster 2a: To apply oil to as part of a religious ceremony. Crosswalk states: To be anointed is to be set apart, empowered, or protected (2 Kings 9:6, 2 Corinthians 1:21–22, James 5:14, Psalm 89:51).

Apocalyptic writing: A form of prophecy that warns us of future events written in symbols and images of what is to come but is hidden from us for the time being. Used in the book of Revelation.

Apostle: A messenger. To be an apostle, it was necessary that they knew Jesus, be witness, and testify of Him from personal knowledge and had been personally selected by Jesus Christ himself. After the death of Jesus, no one can ever take the title of an apostle (John 15:27, Acts 1:21–22, 1 Corinthians 9:1, Acts 22:14–15, Luke 6:13, Galatians 1:1, John 14:26, 16:13, 1 Thessalonians 2:13).

Apocrypha: Ancient religious writings that were not universally accepted or was ultimately rejected as part of the sacred canon that makes up the Bible.

Baptize: New Testament Greek word *baptizo* defines as immersion (https://www.blueletterbible.org). The event of a willing believer to be plunged beneath the water by body and soul into the promise and power of Christ. To be baptized signifies obedience by washing away of our old life and raised into our new and to be made public after the profession of faith by accepting Jesus Christ as savior. The act of baptism does not and cannot save you or wash away your sins (Romans 10:9). It is, however, a very important step of obedience after you have accepted Jesus Christ. It is a symbol of our new life. There are many people in the Bible who died and went to heaven without being baptized (Luke 23:43).

Jesus said in Matthew 28:19 ESV, "Baptizing them in the name of the Father, Son and the Holy Spirit." Some scriptures refer to baptism in the name of Jesus, Lord Jesus or Christ, which is all part of the trinity as stated above and cannot be separated.

BC: Means Before Christ. BC is placed after the year number. *400 BC* meaning four hundred years before Christ. See Fun Facts related to the BC.

Bible: The word Bible comes from the Greek word *Koine* meaning books. The word had the literal meaning of *paper* or *scroll*. The Bible is the Scriptures consisting of the Old Testament and the New Testament.

ca or c: Abbreviated for circa meaning *about* used to indicate approximate dates.

Canon: A biblical canon or canon of scripture is a set of texts or books which a particular Jewish or Christian religious community regards as authoritative scripture. The English word canon comes from the Greek meaning rule or measuring stick. Canon means a criteria by which something is judged.

Century: 100 (hundred) years. A decade is 10 (ten) years.

Christian: Anyone who trusts in Jesus Christ as his or her Savior and who strives to follow his teaching's in every area of life. A person who has been *saved* by accepting the fact that Christ died on the cross for our sins, raised from the dead, and ascended to heaven. Christians are instructed to turn away from their old way of life to live Christ-like. Christians are saved souls, not perfect people.

Christianity: The religion that came from the birth, life, teachings, death, and resurrection of Jesus Christ. Followers and believers of Jesus Christ are called Christians. Christianity is the belief in only one *God* as part of the trinity, the Father, Son, and Holy Spirit. Christianity is not a denomination. "It is the world's largest religion" (Wikipedia.org, Aug 2, 2021).

Covenant: The conditional promises made by God to His people as revealed in Scripture. The agreement between God and the ancient Israelites when God promised to protect them if they kept His law and were faithful to Him. A new covenant was established when Jesus came to earth and the New Testament was created from his teachings.

Denomination: A religious organization where people follow the same beliefs and practices as set in their particular doctrine. A denomination is a religious group which has slightly different beliefs from other groups but within the same faith. A person of Christian faith can follow the teachings of Jesus Christ and the Holy Bible without being under a particular denomination which is called non-denominational. Denominations were created and branched out from the earlier followers of Jesus because humanly speaking, they couldn't agree on certain beliefs or practices. Denominations were not created by God, Jesus, or the Bible.

Disciple: A disciple, originally, were the twelve dedicated followers or students of Jesus Christ. A disciple is someone who believes in Jesus, follows, and seeks to apply His teachings to their daily life.

Epistle: A book of the New Testament in the form of a letter from an apostle. An epistle is a writing directed to a person or group of people usually a formal letter intended to teach. There are twenty-one epistles in the New Testament.

Fasting: Biblical fasting can be defined as not eating food or drink (except water) for a period of time for spiritual purposes. Fasting is a practice of worshiping God (Matthew 6:16–18).

Genre: A class or category having a particular form, style, or content. The word genre is not in the Bible but a term that was used when the Bible was being *put* together. The Bible contains eight different genres: Law, history, wisdom, poetry, gospel, epistles (letters), prophecy, and apocalyptic.

Gentile: A person or group of people that are not Jewish or of Jewish faith.

God: The creator and ruler of the universe and the source of all moral authority. God is one being in three persons. God is the first *person* of the Trinity with the Son and Holy Spirit. He is the author of the Holy Bible. God is all powerful, all-knowing, and all-present. He is everywhere.

Gospel: Gospel means good news. The story of the life, death, and resurrection of Jesus Christ is called the Gospel. The first four books of the New Testament are referred to as the Gospels. The Gospel of Matthew, the Gospel of Mark, the Gospel of Luke, and the Gospel of John are the first four books.

Holy Ghost: Of the modern English translations of the Bible, it is only the King James Version of the Bible which uses the term *Holy Ghost*. It occurs ninety times in the KJV. There is no clear reason why the KJV translators used ghost in most places and then spirit in a few. The exact same Greek and Hebrew words are translated *ghost* and *spirit* in the KJV in different occurrences of the words. In 1611, when the KJV was originally translated, the word *ghost* primarily referred to *an immaterial being*. The Holy Ghost/Holy Spirit is the gift of the Father to His people on earth to initiate and complete the building of the body of Christ (1 Corinthians 12:13). He is also the third part of the Trinity by which the world is convicted of sin, the Lord Jesus is glorified, and believers are transformed into His image (how they live not a physical image) (John 16:7–9; Acts 1:5, 2:4; Romans 8:29; 2 Corinthians 3:18; Ephesians 2:22). See King James. See King James Bible on page 35 in Chapter 3.

Holy Spirit: In Christianity, the third person of the Trinity. The Trinity is the Father, Son, and Holy Spirit. Through the power of the Holy Spirit, believers are saved, filled, and sealed. The Holy Spirit reveals God's thoughts and teaches and guides believers. The Holy Spirit helps Christians in their times of weakness and communicates with God on our behalf. The Holy Spirit is God's presence in the lives of believers. The work of the Holy Spirit in a believer is an ongoing process (Romans 8:10–11, Galatians 5:16–21, and Galatians 5:22–25).

In the Old Testament, the Holy Spirit *came upon* them not *in them*. Example: Judges 15:14, 1 Samuel 10:6–10.

In the New Testament, the Holy Spirit was with Jesus during His ministry.

In the New Testament, Jesus said the Holy Spirit will come after He returns to heaven (John 16:7). The Holy Spirit is the helper. He lives in believers and never leaves (Ephesians 1:13–14).

Interpretation: The action of explaining the meaning of something. To conceive in the light of individual belief, of circumstance, or of judgement.

Jesus Christ: Is the Son of God, the second person of the Trinity. The name Jesus is derived from the Hebrew word Yeshua. The title Christ is the Greek word for Messiah. So Jesus Christ is our Messiah, our Savior. Jesus was born to the Virgin Mary, a Jewish woman, by the Holy Spirit. Joseph was His legal father. Jesus means Savior. Christ means anointed. Anointed is the Greek word for the Hebrew *Messiah*, which is Jesus's title. The New Testament uses the name Jesus Christ about 514 times. The title of Christ which means Messiah is used in the Old Testament as the savior who is to come. Our access to God comes through Jesus Christ.

King James: Born James Stewart in 1566 in Edinburgh, Scotland, and died in 1625. He was the younger cousin of Queen Elizabeth. King James l began his rule as king in 1603 over the Great British Empire. See Fun Facts about how the King James Bible came about.

Manuscript: A book or document written by hand rather than typed or printed. A biblical manuscript is any handwritten copy of text in the bible.

Messiah: From Hebrew meaning *anointed one*. The promised king and deliverer of the Jewish people which was foretold in the Hebrew Bible, the Old Testament. Christians accept Jesus as the Messiah and Savior of mankind.

Messianic: A term used to describe Jewish people who accept Jesus Christ as the Messiah.

New Testament: Is the second part of the Bible which contains the final twenty-seven books also known as scriptures. The books are a collection of gospels, letters (epistles), acts, and prophecy. Written approximately between AD 45 and AD 95. The New Testament is the fulfillment of the promise made by God throughout the Old Testament. The new covenant represented the birth, life, death, and resurrection of Jesus Christ. The New Testament was written in Greek.

Old Testament: The first part of the Bible, containing thirty-nine books or sacred scriptures. It was written approximately 1500 BC to 400 BC. The Old Testament is considered the Bible of the Jewish people. It was the covenant between God and Israel before the arrival of Christ. Written in Hebrew with some Aramaic in the later part of Old Testament history. These scriptures are written of law, history, prophecy, and wisdom.

Papyrus: A material prepared from the stem of a water plant used to make sheets for writing or painting on in ancient Egypt. The word paper comes from papyrus.

Parable: Simple story used by Jesus to illustrate a moral or spiritual lesson.

Pentecost: Comes from the Greek word meaning *fiftieth* (50th). In the Bible, it refers to the Jewish festival that was celebrated fifty days after Passover. The Day of Pentecost marks the beginning of the Christian church. Fifty days after Jesus's death, the Holy Spirit came down on the apostles and miraculously caused them to speak in other languages or tongues so that everyone who came to the festival would hear and understand in their own language (Acts 2:1–13).

Pentateuch: Means the first five books of the Bible. It comes from the Greek word meaning *five books* or *five scrolls*. Archeological discoveries show Moses wrote them.

Pharisee: Was a member of a Jewish religious group who held to the legal and ritual-type traditions. Jesus condemned the Pharisees for being hypocritical in their practices (Matthew 23).

Prayer: Is a conversation with God. Prayer may be oral or mental and from the heart and soul. We do not need to be a speaker or repeat prayers written by someone else to talk with God. It is recommended that we memorize certain prayers to use when needed at particular times in our daily life. If you are new to praying, you can find many beautiful prayers written by others that may express your feelings as well. The Bible is full of prayers that you can say when you have something specific on your heart and are not sure how to express it. The Holy Spirit promises to relay to our Father what we have a difficult time expressing. "...the Holy Spirit also helps in our weakness; for we do not know how to pray as we should, but the Spirit Himself intercedes for us with groaning too deep for words..." (Romans 8:26 NASB).

Prophecy: Is a message communicated to a prophet by God revealing inspiration, interpretation, warnings, or revelations to be shared with the world of events to come.

Prophet: In the Bible, a prophet is a person chosen by God to speak on his behalf to deliver messages or teachings to the people. The Bible states anyone who claims to speak God's words or to teach in his name without being a prophet is a false prophet. Prophets were not chosen by men and could not inherit the title or claim it as official position.

Psalm: A sacred song or hymn in the Bible, mostly in the book of Psalms.

Sadducee: A wealthy *chief priest* who believed God had no role in a person's destiny. They rejected the Pharisees' teachings. The Sadducees were the group with the strongest opposition to Jesus because he was a threat to their erroneous belief system. They were provided political and social benefits by the Roman government. Read Matthew, Mark, Luke, and John.

Salvation: Deliverance or redemption from sin and its consequences also known as *being saved*. To be saved or born again is a total change of heart which comes from the act of accepting the gift of God's grace. Salvation can only be given when you believe and accept Jesus Christ as your Savior (John 3:1–21, Ephesians 2:8, John 3:3, John 3:5–7).

Sanctified: To be set apart for God's special purpose. You can only be sanctified after you have received the offering of Jesus Christ (Hebrews 10:10, Romans 6:19, 1 Thessalonians 4:3)

Saved: By definition, the act of saving or protecting from harm, risk, loss, or destruction. The Bible meaning is deliverance, saving from the power and penalty of sin.

Scribe: Someone who makes written copies of manuscripts and documents before printing was invented. In ancient Israel, scribes were highly-educated, who studied the law and was used to interpret legal documents. The scribe was responsible for preserving the Scripture. They would copy and recopy, counting each letter, word, and spacing to make sure each copy was exact (Ezra 7:6, Matthew 5:20; 12:38).

Scripture: Sacred writings of the Bible.

Scroll: A sheet of parchment or papyrus used for writing on one side and rolled up around a spindle or stick at each end.

Sin: The Christian definition of sin is purposely disobeying the rules of God.

Slave: Hebrew and Greek word is servant or bondman. Slavery (servant) of Judaism was not the cruel system of Greece, Rome, and later nations. The prime thought is service. The servant may render free service, the slave, obligatory, and restricted service. Slaves (servants) were used to pay off their debt, whether monetary or crime. Slaves had to work a set time frame and then could voluntarily stay because the living conditions were better than he/she had before or leave after the debt was paid. Relatives could pay a price to free the *slave*. There are other instances of *slavery* you can find in the Bible. *Slaves* had numerous freedoms and rights during his/her time under a master. Masters were to be punished as well if he caused his *slave* or *bondservant* to be harmed or die under his rule.

Spiritual: Relating to the human spirit or soul. Being spiritual does not always mean you are affiliated with a religion or believe in God and Christianity.

Spiritual gifts: A special ability given to believers by the Holy Spirit to accomplish God's ministry as a whole. "The Spirit has given each of us a special way of serving others. Some of us can speak with wisdom, while others can speak with knowledge, but these gifts come from the same Spirit. To others the Spirit has given great faith or the power to heal the sick or the power to work mighty miracles" (1 Corinthians 12:7–11 ESV). Some of us are prophets, and some of us recognize when God's Spirit is present. Others can speak different kinds of languages, and still others can tell what these languages mean. But it is the Spirit who does all this and decides which gifts to give each of us.

Talent: As used in the Bible, was a form of currency, such as coins or precious metals like silver and gold. A talent was a measuring unit of value used in Greece, Rome, and the Middle East in ancient times (Matthew 25:14–30, 2 Samuel 12:30).

Testament: Something that serves as a sign or evidence of a statement of fact. In the Bible, a testament is the Mosaic old covenant and the Christian new covenant.

Tongue: The Greek term *glossa* meaning language or tongue. Fifty days after Jesus's death, the Holy Spirit (part of the Holy Trinity—Father, Son, and Holy Spirit) came down on the apostles, making them speak in foreign *tongues*. "Every man heard them speak in his own language (tongue)" (Acts 2:6). "Utterly amazed, they asked 'Aren't all these who are speaking, Galileans? Then how is it that each of us hears them in our native language?'" (Acts 2:7–8). Both Jews and converts to Judaism, Cretans and Arabs—we hear them declaring the wonders of God in our own tongues (language) (Acts 2:11). John records: ...And behold, a great multitude, which no one was able to number, out of every nation, tribes, peoples, and "tongues" (languages) (Revelation 7:9).

Translation: Biblical translation is the art and practice of rendering the Bible into languages other than those in which it was originally written.

Trinity: God as three in one: The Father, Son, and Holy Spirit.

Witness: As used in the Old Testament

1.   Evidence or proof (Jeremiah 32:10)
2.   The person who testifies (Leviticus 5:1)

Witness: As used in the New Testament

1.   Record, report, or testimony (1 Timothy 5:19)
2.   One who declares his testimony in his belief in Christ and his teachings (Acts 18:5 and Acts 20:21).

RECOMMENDED SOURCES AND REFERENCE RESOURCES

The resources, books, publications, courses, maps, and other material that I referred to was for inspiration and to ensure the information written in this book is accurate and from reliable sources.

The Holy Bible multiple versions: King James, New Living Translation, Contemporary English Version, New International Version, and English Standard Version.

Chronological Life Application Study Bible: New Living Translation

What the Bible is All About by Dr. Henrietta C. Mears (Forward by Dr. Billy Graham)

The Poverty & Justice Bible: Contemporary English Version

The World's Greatest Book: The Story of How the Bible Came to Be by Lawrence H. Schiffman, PhD, and Jerry Pattengale PhD

How We Got the Bible by Timothy Paul Jones PhD

Bible Resources.org

Our Daily Bread Christian University

How to Study your Bible: A study with Dan Hamel

The #1 Mistake Most Everyone Makes Reading the Bible by Brad Gray

Christianity.com

How to Study the Bible by Robert M. West

Focus on the Family

Answersingenesis.org

Evidence That Demands a Verdict: Life-Changing Truth for a Skeptical World by Josh McDowell

Biblespeak.org: You can listen to audio on how to pronounce words in the Bible. *Free.*

Rose Book of Bible Charts, Maps, and Time Lines

Merriam-Webster Dictionary
https://www.history.com/news/7-things-you-may-not-know-about-the-gutenberg-bible
The Chosen TV series by Dallas Jenkins

Take a look sometime at the website *thisismosaic.org* (make sure it's Winter Garden Florida), and then search for the archive messages, you can find a message on just about any topic about everyday life. That includes sensitive and controversial topics and what the Bible says about them. These sermons will clear up many misunderstandings or confusion about what the Bible says.

In loving memory of
Sam Barnes, who passed away in 1985
My dad, William Edward Taylor, who passed away in 1997
My mom, Maudie Marcella Taylor, who passed away in 2011
My only sister, Joyce F. Taylor-Bentley, who passed away in 2015
My nephew, William "Willy" Taylor, who passed away in 2018

ABOUT THE AUTHOR

Sharon Rose Taylor was born on February 17, 1956, in Oneida, Tennessee, to William and Maudie Taylor (both now gone to be with the Lord). Lived in Cincinnati, Ohio, most of her life, with the exception of a few years in The Villages, Florida. She currently resides in Greenwood, Indiana. Sharon is the sister of six siblings. Starting in order of the first born: James, Joyce (also gone to be with the Lord), Sharon's place in birth order, then Bobby, Benjamin, Jackie, and Jerry. Married David A. Barnes in 1975. From that marriage was born a son James David and a daughter. Her grandchildren from James David and Shaunna are Amelia and Elwood. Her daughter is married and they gave her a granddaughter. In May 2002, she married Sherman Kenner who has two sons, Kyle and Cory, and one daughter, Kasey. She has two other stepdaughters, so with 2 children and 5 step children, she is blessed with lots of grandchildren.

Sharon was born into a home with no spiritual environment until her mom rededicated her life to the Lord in the same time frame that they lived next door to the Barnes family. Sharon was about twelve years old when she first started going to church. Except for her mom, Sam and Nell Barnes had the most Christian influence and were a great inspiration in Sharon's life. Nell continued to be in Sharon's life at the blessed age of ninety-four years old (at the time of writing of this book). Sharon witnessed her mom's love for the Lord Jesus Christ and the endless prayers for her family that never faded. Bill Taylor, her dad, was saved just a short while before he went to be with the Lord.

Sharon's prayer is that the family members that have not accepted Jesus Christ as Savior and have not given their life to the Lord will choose to do so right now.

Education:

Student of Our Daily Bread Christian University. Completed and current courses: Christian Apologetics-Courses: Ten Reasons to Believe in the Bible, Ten Reasons to Believe in Life After Death, Ten Reasons to Believe in the Christian Faith, Biblical Geography Basics, Bible Basics, and Theology Basics.

Studies:

From 2013 to 2018 Bible studies under the leadership of a Messianic-Jewish teacher.

Other Bible studies include: The Book of Revelation; the Book of Daniel, *Here and Now, There and Then;* and the book of David by Beth Moore; *Heaven* by Randy Alcorn; *Joshua* by Barb Roose; *The Armor of God* by Priscilla Shirer; *Uninvited* by Lysa TerKeurst; and *Philippians* by Donald Baker just to name a few over the period of many years.

Below is a short list of the many books that she has read, studied, and currently reading for inspiration to help her prepare for this book.

The World's Greatest Book: The Story of How The Bible Came to Be Authors: L. H. Schiffman, PhD, and Jerry Pattengale, PhD

Evidence That Demands a Verdict: Historical Evidences for the Christian Faith. Author: Josh McDowell

How We Got the Bible. Author: Timothy Paul Jones, PhD

What the Bible Is All About. Author: Dr. Henrietta C. Mears

How to Study the Bible. Author: Robert M. West

Rose Book of Bible Charts, Maps, and Time Lines. Rose Publishing

How Do We Know the Bible is True? Authors: Ken Ham and Bodie Hodge

One Minute After You Die. Author: Erwin W. Lutzer

The Victor Journey Through the Bible. Author V. Gilbert Beers

Heaven. Author: Randy Alcorn

The Chosen. Author: Jerry B. Jenkins

The Bible, several versions, Author: God

Volunteer Experiences:

Midwest Food Bank

Southern Baptist Disaster Relief Team Volunteer: Tornado Joplin Missouri, assisted with clean-up, food distribution, and prayer walk.

Southern Baptist Disaster Relief Chainsaw Team Volunteer: Hurricane, meal distribution in partnership with the Red Cross, tree removal, and debris clean-up

2007 Venezuela with International Mission Board

2008 Educational Tour of Israel with Global Mission Ministry

2012 Haiti, Hands and Feet Orphan Ministry

2013 Haiti, My Life Speaks Orphan Ministry

CPSIA information can be obtained
at www.ICGtesting.com
Printed in the USA
LVHW071441120722
723335LV00023B/1006